Martin Kramer, *University of California, Berkeley*
EDITOR-IN-CHIEF

Using Consultants Successfully

Jon F. Wergin
Virginia Commonwealth University

EDITOR

Number 73, Spring 1991

JOSSEY-BASS INC., PUBLISHERS
San Francisco

USING CONSULTANTS SUCCESSFULLY
Jon F. Wergin (ed.)
New Directions for Higher Education, no. 73
Volume XIX, number 1
Martin Kramer, Editor-in-Chief

Microfilm copies of issues and articles are available in 16mm and 35mm, as well as microfiche in 105mm, through University Microfilms Inc., 300 North Zeeb Road, Ann Arbor, Michigan 48106.

LC 85-644752   ISSN 0271-0560   ISBN 1-55542-789-8

NEW DIRECTIONS FOR HIGHER EDUCATION is part of The Jossey-Bass Higher and Adult Education Series and is published quarterly by Jossey-Bass Inc., Publishers (publication number USPS 990-880). Second-class postage paid at San Francisco, California, and at additional mailing offices. Postmaster: Send address changes to Jossey-Bass Inc., Publishers, 350 Sansome Street, San Francisco, California 94104.

EDITORIAL CORRESPONDENCE should be sent to the Editor-in-Chief, Martin Kramer, 2807 Shasta Road, Berkeley, California 94708.

Cover photograph and random dot by Richard Blair/Color & Light © 1990.

Printed on acid-free paper in the United States of America.

CONTENTS

EDITOR'S NOTES

The use of consultants is a relatively new phenomenon in American higher education. As recently as the late 1970s Pilon and Bergquist wrote, "Consultation seems to be particularly difficult for those working with colleges and universities because there is little or no precedent in these institutions for consultative assistance" (1979, p. 6).

That statement could not be made today. Needs and opportunities created in the last twenty years, first by increased federal support of higher education (such as Title III), then by federal and state regulations (such as "outcomes assessment"), have led to such a widespread use of consultants that today specialized consultant expertise is available in areas as diverse as student recruitment, computing, and organizational development.

Now, as many institutions face serious budgetary challenges, finding cost-effective ways of using institutional consultants has become even more important. While literally scores of books have been written to assist the prospective consultant, few guides are available to help the institutional client.

This volume has been put together to help fill that void. In it the campus administrator will find practical advice on when to use consultants, where to find them, how to identify those most capable of addressing the institution's problems, and how to work with consultants to effect meaningful and constructive change.

The chapters have been written by authors with extensive experience on both sides of the desk. They include current and former college presidents, heads of educational consulting firms, and association officers. (By the way, I am none of these; I have simply done some research on the subject and have worked as a consultant to several institutions, mostly on evaluation issues.) Topics in the book have been arranged to correspond roughly to stages of the consultation process. In Chapter One Daniel H. Pilon surveys the development of consultation in higher education and forecasts how institutions might use consultants most profitably in the 1990s. In Chapter Two I suggest several questions to raise prior to deciding whether to engage a consultant; in effect, the chapter is intended to help the reader decide whether to read further. In Chapter Three Russell Garth and Mary Ann Rehnke describe ways of using available consultant networks in higher education and suggest several creative low-cost alternatives for gaining an external perspective on the problem. In Chapter Four George Dehne offers some detailed suggestions on selecting the right person or firm for the task, including writing the request for proposal, setting the criteria for selection, and matching candidates' credentials with institutional needs. In Chapter Five Lynn Curry discusses the specifics of negotiating the actual contract and includes examples of the types of contracts that

NEW DIRECTIONS FOR HIGHER EDUCATION, no. 73, Spring 1991 © Jossey-Bass Inc., Publishers

may be entered into. In Chapter Six Willard F. Enteman focuses on the heart of the consultation itself: ways the campus administrator can manage the consultancy and its immediate aftermath to take best advantage of what the consultant has to offer. In Chapter Seven Jack Lindquist offers a lively commentary on using consultants' feedback to avoid the dreaded "dusty report syndrome" (my term, not his). Finally, in Chapter Eight Robert J. Toft addresses a topic not often covered in works like this— namely, how to view a consultancy as a stimulant for long-term institutional change. At the end of the book is a short annotated list of useful references.

A brief comment concerning definitions and style is appropriate. First, who exactly is a "consultant"? The general definition employed here is perhaps more limited than that used in other works. For the purposes of this book a *consultant* is someone external to the institution who is brought on campus temporarily or intermittently for the primary purpose of giving advice or facilitating resolution of a local problem or issue. This definition does not include hired help brought in to replace staff members temporarily or to relieve an episodic overload of work. In short, under this definition consultants help an institution decide what to do; they do not carry out day-to-day responsibilities. Second, these chapters have been written specifically for the academic administrator: they are directed to those on campus who are most likely to retain consulting services. The terms *campus administrator, dean,* and *president* will be found throughout the text and should each be interpreted generically. Third, sexist language has been avoided by using male and female pronouns randomly and interchangeably. The reader should not infer a particular referent by the use of one or the other.

If the contributors to this volume share a common message, it is this: Be clear about what you want, be open about your expectations, and be firm in your management of the process. And never, ever, lose sight of your larger goals.

Jon F. Wergin
Editor

Reference

Pilon, D. H., and Bergquist, W. H. *Consultation in Higher Education: A Handbook for Practitioners and Clients.* Washington, D.C.: Council of Independent Colleges, 1979.

Jon F. Wergin is director of the Center for Educational Development and Faculty Resources at Virginia Commonwealth University in Richmond.

Consultants and higher education clients have worked together for many years. The rapidly changing landscape of American higher education has produced continuing evolution in consulting practice as well as in the areas consultants serve.

Emerging Needs for Consultants in Higher Education

Daniel H. Pilon

Despite many snide one-liners ("a consultant is someone from fifty miles away with a briefcase" or "a consultant is someone who borrows your watch and tells you what time it is"), consultants have provided needed expertise in a timely, efficient, and cost-effective manner to institutions of higher education for many years. However, the patterns of consultant use by colleges and universities have developed and shifted significantly over the past three decades and most likely will shift again in the years to come. In this introductory chapter I will discuss the evolution of the use of consultants in higher education and will suggest some of the underlying conditions that have shaped those patterns of use. In this context I will offer some thoughts about the uses that colleges and universities may be expected to make of consultants in the years to come.

Roles Consultants Play

Consultants make it possible for organizations with limited resources to obtain high-powered expertise on an as-needed basis. Consultants also provide objective assessments of complex situations and assistance in processing change in an organization. Even though the cost per hour or per day for a consultant may far exceed what an institution pays any of its full-time employees, the time frame of the consulting engagement is circumscribed, and the financial exposure of the client is therefore far more limited than it would be if a full-time employee were added to the payroll.

In some cases, consultants respond to needs that have been with colleges and universities for many years but for which it does not make

NEW DIRECTIONS FOR HIGHER EDUCATION, no. 73, Spring 1991 © Jossey-Bass Inc., Publishers

sense to hire full-time professionals. For example, only the largest institutions can afford full-time staff personnel who are professional architects; similarly, for smaller institutions legal expertise is most often provided by outside counsel rather than an in-house attorney. However, even in large institutions where both staff architects and legal counsel are found, outside consultants still find their way in to meet special needs and situations.

In other cases, there is regular need for outside expertise no matter what the level of internal resources. External financial auditing and accreditation reviews are cases in point. Other examples might include the assessment of a college's or university's ability to undertake a major fund-raising effort or perhaps a performance review of top-level administrators. Often the objectivity or fresh perspective provided by an outsider is a critical factor in achieving reliable results in each of these areas.

Still other situations requiring a consultant may arise suddenly. Resolving a complex community relations problem, handling the results of a toxic waste spill, or perhaps investigating allegations of impropriety of a key official are examples. Another occasion fitting this paradigm is the sudden departure of a key person. Consultants can also be engaged as temporary replacements (for example, as an acting president) or as part of the effort to identify and hire an appropriate successor.

Changes in federal or state statutes or regulations may also lead to the enlistment of consultants who can advise the institution regarding its changing responsibilities and help devise appropriate record-keeping mechanisms. The recent effort to ensure equity in fringe benefits (Section 89 of the Internal Revenue Code) is one example. Colleges and universities rushed to acquire new computer software and consulting advice to ensure that they were in compliance. Ironically, soon after most institutions accomplished the required reviews, many of the provisions of Section 89 were deferred or repealed.

Other needs for consultants have evolved with changes in circumstances. For example, as competition for capable students has become more intense among colleges and universities, the number of consultants in the admissions-recruitment-retention field has increased rapidly. Similarly, as institutions have become increasingly dependent on philanthropy for their overall success, consulting firms and individual consultants have thrived. Not only does the traditional consultation with respect to the overall fund-raising process continue but also increased specialization continues to grow. Some consultants restrict their services to the development of fund-raising letters. Others offer editing services that are only as far away as the nearest facsimile machine. Still others deal with specific aspects of deferred giving and prospect research and file management.

Elements in Successful Consultation

While there are many needs that can be met effectively through the use of consultants, there are at least three other factors that enter the equation and will affect the ultimate outcome. One element is the availability of capable consultants; another is the availability of resources to pay for consultants' services; a third (discussed in later chapters) is the client's ability to define the problem and use the results of the consultation.

A cursory review of the mail for a week or two in any college president's office offers a better understanding of the almost unbelievable number of persons willing to provide consulting assistance either on the campus or through workshops and other activities. However, determining which of the possibilities will actually provide quality services and where to find the resources to support them is often less obvious. Dollars for consultants must come from either the college's own operating budget or outside sources. As with other expenditures, the institution must be convinced that a particular consulting relationship is the best possible use of limited dollars. Often there is considerable competition among needs. When institutional dollars are committed, however, the likelihood that the advice sought will be put to good use is substantially enhanced.

The consultant is certainly a critical element in the equation. There are, however, wide variations in quality among those who claim to be "consultants." Later chapters in this volume deal with determining the extent of the real need for consultants as well as means of finding the "right consultant." Both matters are important and, if they are given sufficient attention, can help save prospective clients from wasted and even counterproductive uses of dollars and precious time.

Historical Development of Consulting in Higher Education

Although many think of the late 1960s and the 1970s as the time when consultants began to have a major impact on higher education, consultants have, in fact, made their mark for a much longer period. Whether one considers the role of architects in campus planning or the visitation of consultant-evaluators from one or another of the regional accrediting associations (begun by the North Central Association as early as 1906–1907) or even the annual visit from accountants as part of the auditing process, consultants have had an impact on higher education since early in the century.

As mentioned at the outset, attorneys, accountants, architects, and accrediting agencies represented the most common early uses of consultants by colleges and universities. These professionals brought (and continue to bring) specialized expertise to the campus, enabling clients to deal with specific problems and to authenticate institutional assertions regarding academic integrity and financial health.

The next major addition to the consulting world came with the fund-raising "campaigners." These individuals and organizations provided the expertise to plan and often to run fund-raising drives. Fund-raising counsel continues to be a major area of consultation used by institutions of higher education of all sizes. The process has become increasingly sophisticated, and there are certainly many more sellers of the service than in years past. Consultation related to fund-raising is basic from the perspective of both institutional need and available consulting resources.

In the 1950s increasing interest in the combination of institutional planning and fund-raising developed. Perceptive practitioners began to view the two areas as integral to one another, and a number of national consulting firms grew out of the association of individuals who had experience and expertise that they wished to share in these fields. Many early consultants were persons nearing retirement or perhaps late in their careers and seeking new challenges. While there were surely many others, the Gonzer, Gerber, Tinkur, and Stuhr firm as well as Frantzreb and Pray come immediately to mind. These groups and others like them were concerned about institutional advancement issues, but they also worked toward strengthening the total institution as a part of the process. There was also some reflection in this process on the importance of planning for the future, a notion that was then becoming more prominent in the corporate world.

As the use of consultants widened in the business world, trustees and regents of colleges and universities began to bring their experiences with consultants into the academic world. As a result, by the 1960s outside consultants were increasingly used in the hiring process. As part of the screening process, it was not unusual to send applicants for significant positions to a consulting psychologist for a personality profile (a practice that would now be of dubious legality in all but the most carefully planned and criterion-referenced instances). Professional search consultants (the so-called headhunters) also began to make their impact in the marketplace.

The explosion of the use of consultants in higher education came during the 1960s and 1970s. These were volatile years in many ways. There was rapid technological development, funds were increasingly available from outside sources to support the purchase of consulting services, external funding agencies often stipulated that programs given grant support undergo external evaluation, marketing was becoming an increasingly important part of the administrative process as students became (or were expected to become) more scarce, and in some cases there were needs for consultants regarding closure or mergers of institutions.

On the technological side, the computer as an administrative tool made an abrupt entrance into the educational world just as it did in many other areas of American business and commerce. Once the computer arrived, its applications and capabilities mushroomed. With that growth came ample opportunities for consultation regarding equipment choice, software design, and use of the large quantities of data being churned out. *Management information system* was becoming a catch phrase.

With the growing availability of complex and easily manipulated data bases came a growing interest in organizational planning, again a reflection of what was occurring in the business world. Needs, with respect to both long-range planning and management information systems, were stimulated for smaller institutions by the Strengthening Developing Institutions Program (Title III, Higher Education Act, or HEA), which made attention to both areas essential elements in any proposal that would receive support.

The Title III program did even more to stimulate consulting relationships. In addition to mandating planning and management activities in proposals with a hope of being funded, it also required external evaluation and, in the early years, something called a "cooperative relationship" with a more developed institution or organization. Such relationships really involved consultation by "experts" from the cooperating institution to the grantee. This brought institutions that were far beyond "developing" themselves under the influence of the consulting boom as well, if not as users, then as providers.

Finally, because Title III in its various evolutionary stages involved substantial amounts of money (grants to individual colleges in excess of $1 million over a few years' time were the norm), another consulting area evolved related to the application for such grants. Several consulting firms and groups began to specialize in helping prospective grantees apply for support with the understanding that the consulting firm would then provide services if the proposal was successful.

It is not too much to suggest that perhaps one of the single largest causes of the boom in the use of consultants in the smaller colleges was the evolution of Title III. Other major programs contributing to the boom were the Trio Programs, the Cooperative Education Program, and the College Science Improvement Program (COSIP) administered by the National Science Foundation. In all of these federally supported efforts were plenty of opportunities (and money) to hire consultants.

While some of the areas of consultation that follow were also tied to Title III projects, each also attracted interest in and of its own right. By the late 1960s and early 1970s the college admissions process was undergoing a dramatic change. The advent of significant numbers of community colleges and the evolution of many normal schools into teacher's colleges and then into regional universities created many more opportunities for good students. The availability of financial aid, often from both federal and state sources as well as from institutional coffers, combined with declining birthrates to create a buyer's market. With the "crisis" in admissions came increasing interest in obtaining what might best be described as sales and marketing expertise to help make a particular institution more attractive than its competitors. This part of the consulting business has continued to grow and develop and continues to thrive today.

From consulting in recruitment it was just a quick step to consulting related to retention. The appearance of Robert Cope and William Hannah's *Revolving College Doors* (1975) and Alexander Astin's *Preventing Students from Dropping Out* in the same year helped a growing number of institutions understand the importance of defining and resolving student attrition problems. At the same time a number of practitioners willing to unwrap the mysteries of successful retention programs appeared on the scene. Retention continues to be a matter of considerable interest.

As mentioned earlier, a phenomenon that reached higher education from its early development in the business world was the use of headhunters (as opposed to employment agencies) to conduct searches for staff members and faculty at all levels. This consultative process became especially fine-tuned with respect to the search for college and university presidents. One of the earliest efforts in this regard began under the egis of the Association of American Colleges and continues as the Academic Search Consultation Service. This consulting role, like many others mentioned in this chapter, also continues through for-profit organizations and independent consultants and often provides a valuable service. Consultants help institutions define their personnel needs, make sure that all appropriate resources are tapped, and work to ensure that screening and interviewing take place in a rational and legal way and that the final hiring process reaches an amicable solution.

Consultants are also used increasingly in personnel training roles, as inspirational and informational speakers for faculty institutes, and to help groups of persons in institutions do their jobs more effectively. Much of the growth in this area can be traced to the faculty development movement in the late 1960s, which continued (albeit with less formality) well into the 1980s. Experts on teaching, faculty life planning, evaluation, and every aspect of the teaching process and learning styles were brought to campuses for institutes and even for consultation with individual faculty members to help prepare growth plans and other devices designed to breathe fresh life into the many faculty members in a number of critical fields who suddenly found themselves placebound by the glut of new Ph.D. degree holders.

One additional area that emerged during the boom years and in which consultant services began to be used more widely is the general area of conflict resolution. The notion that the outside expert, the objectifier, the arbitrator, the peacemaker could be an important contributor to building community was again borrowed from corporate America.

Consultants: An Expanding Resource Base

The fact that consultants were needed and that resources (often in abundance) were available to support their work led to a similar growth in the number of persons and organizations who offered their services as consultants. While the firms that had provided some of the service (particularly with respect to fund-raising) continued as in the past, many new consultants and consulting organizations appeared on the scene.

In many cases the evolution from practitioner to consultant was rapid. A college or university person in need of assistance would often tap into an informal network of acquaintances and perhaps professional organizations to find a person who was knowledgeable or experienced in that particular area. The persons selected to provide consulting services to other institutions of higher education were often "field-trained generals," and there was often an assumption that if one knew enough about something or performed a particular role effectively, one could consult about it effectively as well. Satisfaction on the part of one client would often produce more clients and a modest consulting practice for a person otherwise employed as a faculty member or administrator. This pattern is similar to that by which faculty began to develop consulting practices with business, industry, and other organizations. It was not unusual for academic departments in major universities to organize into consulting groups to respond to extramural opportunities.

Persons working as part-time consultants sometimes found the consulting world sufficiently attractive and lucrative to consider making consulting their full-time work. Persons drawn to this arrangement were often late in their careers and interested in keeping active while avoiding full-time employment. Others were successful practitioners with good consulting track records who were drawn to full-time consulting by groups or firms in the consulting business. This occurred in a number of situations when organizations with consulting practices in general business management wanted to break into the increasingly lucrative college and university consulting business.

During this period of rapid growth there were some attempts to train consultants as well as to develop networks for consultants under the umbrella of a variety of voluntary organizations. One such arrangement is the Professional and Organizational Development Network (known simply as POD), which runs its own conferences and training programs and even produces its own newsletter. In general, however, a sort of free market system functioned and continues to function today.

One of the more interesting efforts to network, train, and evaluate consultants was developed through the efforts of the Council for the Advancement of Small Colleges (CASC, now known as the Council of Independent Colleges or CIC) with the support of the Kellogg Foundation. This effort was designed to identify skilled practitioners and train them in consulting skills and techniques and to bring together colleges with needs and available talent; the network also evaluated the work as it was completed. Because the consulting network was designed to help colleges help themselves, it provided services at minimal costs and paid participating consultants very modest fees. *Consultation in Higher Education: A Handbook for Practitioners and Clients* (Pilon and Bergquist, 1979) was produced as a result of that project. During the most fertile years of the Title III program the consulting network, along with many similar groups, functioned effectively alongside the profit-oriented consulting services.

Clients Learn, Too

As part of the boom period in consulting, several important things happened. Colleges and universities came to know the positive value that consultants could bring to their existence. They also learned that using consultants was an acquired skill, as was the process of identifying needs for consultation in the first place. Many users of consultants came to a better understanding of the real cost of consultation, which included not just the fee and expenses of the consultant but also the many hours of preparation for and participation in the consultancy by institutional personnel to ensure its success. If anything, an understanding of this cost issue has contributed to making many colleges and universities more careful and more selective as they consider possible consultant roles.

As a result of the use of consultants on a somewhat regular basis, many institutions came to understand that not all consultants are created equal. Some consultants were "solutions in search of problems." They knew and understood one set of responses to a problem but were unable to tailor what they knew to different environments. In other cases, unfortunately, the skills that made one an effective practitioner in some areas were the ones that caused a lack of success in others. Someone who is a decisive "doer" on his or her own campus may have trouble adjusting to being a "listener-processor" who will help the clients solve their own problems.

Changing Times: Changing Needs

As the 1980s came to a close, the volume of consulting work was declining somewhat and there was a shift in the areas in which consultants' expertise was used. This is a natural enough phenomenon. Some needs are met while changing circumstances cause new needs to develop. For example, computers and sophisticated management information systems have become de rigueur for most colleges. Questions surrounding computer expansion and enhancements are most often worked out with vendors and on-campus personnel. Likewise, for most institutions, some sort of long-range planning process is in place and functional. While it may be appropriate to fine-tune the process from time to time, the once common consulting engagement designed to help an institution adopt and implement a planning strategy is found far less frequently today.

Some consulting situations can be expected to continue. Consultants frequently simplify the development of new programs and curricula. Likewise, the use of consultants in the various institutional and specialized program accrediting processes will continue. It is reasonable to expect that these processes will become more sophisticated (for example, the increased emphasis on outcomes measurement as part of the accrediting review) and that the quality of the consulting aspect of the process will improve. Training programs for those involved in these important roles are becoming more commonplace. (The North Central Association currently provides training opportunities for its "consultant-evaluators" and will shortly begin requiring training for its "team chairs.") Likewise, some of the approaches to the consulting/evaluation visits are also becoming more sensitive and creative. The emphasis on outcomes evaluation criteria rather than input measures is growing.

Consultation with architects, attorneys, and accountants will also continue. Again, the level of sophistication with regard to the kinds of help available and the ability of the client institutions to use the help effectively seems to be on the rise. National accounting and management consulting firms with multiple clients in the higher education world, for example, are beginning to provide better comparative data for clients.

New situations are emerging. In some measure many recent developments in consulting reflect not so much new problems as increasingly sophisticated and specialized methods of managing old ones. What was originally an attempt to help with admissions or recruiting work by developing simple, effective systems has evolved into an extremely complex and specialized field where many organizations practice and provide a variety of consulting help. Work ranges from sophisticated telemarketing schemes and the design of direct mail materials to total admissions programs where companies actually become, in effect, the admissions office for the college or university. Training programs for admissions staff personnel are common both on campus (in the case of larger institutions) and at centralized locations.

Similarly, sophistication is developing in the area of attracting philanthropic support. Consultants who work with "prospect research" and computerized "prospect management systems" are common. Much consulting work continues in the area of deferred giving. With the ever increasing competition for gifts via direct mail, ample help is available in that area as well. Specialists who edit fund-raising materials (quickly transmitted from place to place by computer modem and facsimile machines) advertise in the fund-raising periodicals. A brochure that recently crossed this writer's desk touted the availability of a consultant who would actually accompany a college staff person or volunteer on the call to ask for a major gift.

To some extent, future needs will also be shaped by situations that emerge. As noted earlier, the appearance of Section 89 regulations prompted a flurry of activity. Similar results can reasonably be expected if and when new demands are made for reports on such matters as graduation, place-ment, and campus crime statistics. Recent actions by Congress requiring institutional alcohol and drug policy statements as well as plans for dealing with alcohol and drug problems as a condition for receiving federal support will be important catalysts leading to consulting relationships. Consultants can be expected to offer services ranging from the development of systems to collect needed data to methods for improving an individual college's suc-cess or achievement rates in dealing with the various issues.

Continuing concern with fringe benefits has also produced much consulting activity. While the Section 89 issues are at least temporarily on hold, other matters, including health insurance, are receiving more notice. Questions about controlling health care costs, for example, are critical as the impact of rising health care prices is felt by institutions that provide health care coverage to employees. Likewise, with the growing number of options and the often contradictory advice and claims of the various pro-viders of retirement programs, institutions are finding it more necessary to obtain the advice of impartial sources as they try to find equitable and affordable options.

Maintenance of the physical plant is also becoming a demanding area. Years of deferring important campus maintenance projects in order to channel dollars into seemingly more pressing areas have produced serious problems for many campuses. The need to plan and implement "catch-up" programs that are efficient, cost-effective, and reflective of appropriate priorities often requires the professional advice of the objec-tive outsider.

With the break-up of the telephone monopoly and general deregula-tion in the telephone-communications area, many colleges and universities have gone to outside assistance to sort through the plethora of options that continue to appear. Each passing month seems to bring additional alterna-tives and concomitant claims of increased efficiency and big dollar savings. Institutions are seeking help as they try to evaluate claims and settle on systems that will really meet their needs.

Another area of recent concern has involved the management (and hopefully elimination) of racial and ethnic tension and sexism on cam-puses across the nation. This is an area that drew considerable attention in the 1960s, waned, and has now unfortunately returned to the forefront. Skilled consultants often play effective roles in promoting increased under-standing and developing plans for alleviating tensions that already exist on individual campuses.

In short, it might be suggested that any time a situation viewed as threat-ening or puzzling appears, there will be consultants who will respond and market their services to potential clients. This marks a significant change from when the use of consultants first became a normal way of responding in such situations. Earlier, institutions usually spent a great deal of time and effort trying to identify appropriate consultants. Today, if anything, the difficulty is to choose among those who stand ready to help.

To choose effectively, institutions must learn a great deal about themselves, the consulting process, and those who offer consulting services. The chapters that follow address these and other issues. Because of the expense in terms of human energy as well as financial commitment, it is essential that colleges and universities continue to hone their abilities to use the talents of those who offer to serve them.

References

Astin, A. W. *Preventing Students from Dropping Out.* San Francisco: Jossey-Bass, 1975.

Cope, R., and Hannah, W. *Revolving College Doors: The Causes and Consequences of Dropping Out, Stopping Out and Transferring.* New York: Wiley, 1975.

Pilon, D. H., and Bergquist, W. H. *Consultation in Higher Education: A Handbook for Practitioners and Clients.* Washington, D.C.: Council of Independent Colleges, 1979.

Daniel H. Pilon has been president of the College of St. Scholastica in Duluth, Minnesota, since 1981. Prior to coming to St. Scholastica, he was vice-president for campus services and director of the National Consulting Network at the Council of Independent Colleges.

Before committing to the expense of a consultancy, the college
administrator needs to consider several basic questions related to
purpose, risk, and cost.

Do You Really Need a Consultant?

Jon F. Wergin

In the previous chapter Daniel Pilon outlined a variety of ways in which colleges and universities may use consultants. At first glance the question posed as the title to this chapter may thus seem superfluous, and the answer to it obvious: simply find and hire a consultant whenever faced with one of the "emerging situations" about which Pilon talks. But of course the decision is much more complicated than that, and before plunging ahead a little self-diagnosis is in order. In this chapter I will offer some guidelines to help answer this basic question: What can I reasonably expect a consultant to do for me that I cannot do for myself? More particularly: What is the problem for which I need assistance? What is keeping my own staff from solving the problem? I will address these last two questions in turn.

What Is the Problem?

Those who are in the business of giving advice to the "clients" of consultants, both in business and industry (Schein, 1987; Holtz, 1989) and in higher education (Matthews, 1983; Wergin, 1989), have suggested a number of problems that might appear to benefit from consultant expertise. The following are some of them.

An Ad Hoc Project or Crisis that Requires a Highly Specialized Level of Knowledge, Skill, or Experience. This is probably the most obvious reason for hiring a consultant: you need specific *technical* expertise that lies well beyond the capabilities of campus staff, and you need it only temporarily. You have diagnosed the problem, and you need a specialist to write the appropriate prescription. Using consultants in this way presupposes that you have defined the problem correctly, that you have been able to identify the appropriate expertise required, that you are able to communicate the problem correctly to the consultant, and that you are prepared to accept the consequences of whatever prescription the consultant writes for you (Schein, 1987). As Pilon and Dehne note elsewhere in this volume, consultants in higher education are becoming increasingly specialized in the way they market their services; therefore, the campus administrator who decides preemptively what the problem is and what needs to be done about it risks buying a solution to the wrong problem.

A Need to Lend External Credence to an Already Identified Course of Action. This is arguably the *worst* reason to hire a consultant. In my study of consultation projects sponsored by the Association of American Colleges (Wergin, 1989), I discovered that in several cases consultants were brought in to help justify and implement solutions previously identified by the campus administration. Without exception, consultants engaged at this stage were viewed by the faculty as political tools of the administration, brought on campus to help ramrod unpopular policies. Using consultants to help garner political support for a path already chosen—particularly if it is a distasteful one, such as budget retrenchment—can have consequences opposite to those intended. When faced with difficult decisions, therefore, it is far better to bring in consultants early and use them to help facilitate discussion and outline alternatives and probable consequences.

A Need for an Outside, Disinterested Opinion on Potential Courses of Action. In contrast to the previous problem, consultants may be very useful here. The situation is analogous to a patient asking for a second opinion of a diagnosis or approach to medical treatment. An outsider with some credibility to the campus community (for example, someone from a sister institution who has faced a similar problem before) can play devil's advocate, questioning assumptions and generally cross-examining the logic behind presumed cause-effect relationships (for example, by asking, "What led you to think that doing X would cause Y to result?"). This kind of critique can be extremely useful, especially if the options being considered are costly, critical to the survival or financial health of the institution, or involve substantial risk (Holtz, 1989). Suppose, for example, that a small college were considering a proposal to implement a nontraditional studies program aimed at older, part-time students. An external consultant—someone, of course, who has not participated in the development of the plan—could review the plan and the premises on which it was based and ask some fundamental questions related to need, market, competition, cost, and perceived internal and external political support.

Changing Institutional Responsibilities. In Chapter One, Daniel Pilon discussed how useful, even necessary, consultants can be in helping the institution respond to changing external requirements. Until recently, this has applied more to public than private institutions; however, the face of higher education is changing in the direction of greater bureaucratic control over the independents as well. The issue of institutional assessment is a good example. Assessment as a national movement in higher education appears to be here to stay and has kept those who have expertise in curricular and program evaluation busy as consultants to campuses large and small. Accrediting bodies, too, are requiring increasingly greater documentation of students' learning outcomes as part of an institution's self-study document. Consultants can play a most useful role in helping the institution develop and implement assessment plans that not only meet the state's mandate but also provide information useful internally for program improvement.

"Sensitive" Investigations. This problem and the following one present two ways consultants can perform useful functions that are overtly political. In each case, consultants may be used to help defuse the politics by acting as disinterested third parties having no vested interest in the local issue. Here, consultants may be used to conduct an "impartial" investigation of a particularly sensitive issue on campus: the differential tenure status of minority faculty members, for example, or the involvement of alumni in the college's athletic program. I put the term *impartial* in quotation marks because no such investigation, no matter how impeccable the investigator's credentials, can be or can be assumed to be objective or free from bias. The most one can hope for is that the consultant's report will inform the debate. I should add also that administrators using consultants in this way must recognize the political risks involved: they are relinquishing at least part of their control over the process to an outsider who may or may not provide the political ammunition they need to take the course of action they most desire. Any perception that the administrator is using the consultant to manipulate the process will likely backfire, as I pointed out earlier.

Controversial Campus Issues. In the Association of American Colleges (AAC) study (Wergin, 1989), I found this to be one of the most useful functions of consultants. Sometimes campus issues become so controversial that factions become mired in their positions. Most common here are issues such as academic reorganization or program initiatives that can be implemented only with a concomitant reduction in other areas. In one example from the AAC study, consultants were called in to evaluate a new campus writing program. As this observer noted, the consultant teams' *mediating* role turned out to be more useful than their initial *evaluation* role: "Overall the effect was excellent. The consultants were patient, aware of the delicacy of the situation, and asked serious questions. They listened carefully to faculty and were able to consolidate what faculty said into a coherent set of recommendations. The team was able to show how the immediate issues reflected long-range problems. They pulled no punches, and their intellectual honesty helped defuse the political environment" (Wergin, 1989, p. 8).

A Long-Standing, Chronic Problem. This is another consultant function highlighted as most effective in the AAC study (Wergin, 1989). In contrast to the previous problem, which encompasses primarily acute political crises, this one deals more with chronic problems that are so large or complex that internal efforts at resolution have proved futile, and campus administrators and faculty members have become tired and frustrated. Examples could include such large issues as major curriculum reform and the development of useful long-range or strategic planning. In these cases consultants may be able to reenergize the effort and focus that energy on accomplishable goals. Particularly if consultants are hired as part of a grant-funded project, they can serve as catalysts for campus action by spotlighting the task at hand and giving it a certain immediacy. Simply knowing that consultants will visit the campus periodically constitutes an incentive for action and provides needed momentum. Finally, skillful consultants can help reduce institutional resistance to change. As a campus respondent at one of the colleges in the AAC study said, "By addressing faculty concerns with a wealth of experience and insight, [the consultant] was able to cut through fear of change and suspicion of planning" (Wergin, 1989, p. 19).

Problem Definition. I have saved this occasion for using consultants for last, in part because of its apparent irony. One might think it foolish to seek the help of a consultant without having already defined specifically what problem the consultant is supposed to solve, and yet a consultant can often be *most* helpful when the problem is not well defined at all. The usefulness of consultants in the early stages of problem definition has been well documented from a host of diverse settings (Schein, 1987; Holtz, 1989; Wergin, 1989). While all agree that the ultimate success of a consultation depends on how accurately the problem is identified and defined, the difficulty is that "problems" ("causes") are often hard to distinguish from "symptoms" ("effects")—vague dissatisfactions with general education requirements, for example—and campus administrators are often too close to the situation to tell the difference.

One of the primary benefits of a consultation, then, can be to help define the problem. Schein (1969) has referred to this form of consultation as "process consultation," which he defines this way: "The manager's real problem often is that he *does not know* what he is looking for, and, indeed, should not really be expected to know. All he knows is that something is not right. An important part of the consultation process is to help the manager or the organization define what the problem is, and only then decide what further kind of help is needed" (p. 18).

In his most recent book, Schein (1987) has listed several criteria that might help indicate whether process consultation is likely to be helpful. For each of these I have suggested an example from a higher education context: *The source of the problem is unknown.* Contributions from alumni have declined in recent years.

The kind of help that is needed or available is unknown. The administrator is unsure whether to put more campus resources into marketing, financial aid packages, or both.

The client is likely to benefit from the process of diagnosis. A college president is feeling pressure from the board of trustees, who feel that the college is losing its marketability to traditional college-age students.

The consultant is to be hired with "constructive intent." The campus administrator is truly looking for fresh perspectives, not simply an external point of view to buttress her own.

The client is the only one who knows what will work. The administrator understands that the consultant will be expected not to *solve* her problem but rather to help her and her campus colleagues make more informed choices.

Perhaps the very first step, then, is to acknowledge the ambiguity: to resist feelings of embarrassment about calling in a consultant without a clearly defined problem agenda. As Holtz (1989) has pointed out, it is self-defeating to overlook the consultant's perspective on the situation, and it is dangerous to compromise possible creative solutions by phrasing the problem in a way that would restrict the alternatives.

How, then, does one know when the "real" problem has been identified? Holtz (1989) has suggested a useful rule of thumb: "The problem has been identified when it contains within its definition a direct clue to the solution, to a set of probable solutions, or (at least) to a direct approach to a solution" (p. 39).

Consider the following example. Suppose that as dean of a liberal arts college you are troubled by what you perceive to be the reluctance of college faculty to implement recently adopted general education requirements, even though these requirements have already been endorsed by the appropriate faculty committees and the collegewide faculty senate. Does "faculty reluctance to implement requirements" qualify as an appropriate statement of the problem? Probably not: what you are perceiving is likely a symptom that could have several underlying causes, each of which implies a different kind of solution. The faculty may be unaware of how the requirements affect their own departmental programs, they may be aware of the need for curriculum changes but not know how to make them, they may have perceptions different from yours about the extent of change required, and so forth. Note how each one of these possibilities, if true, implies a particular intervention strategy that may be taken.

To summarize: one of the most useful functions of a consultant is to help define the problem more precisely. It is important, however, that the college administrator be clear that this activity will be part of the consultancy.

What Is Keeping My Own Staff from Solving the Problem?

While good consultants can perform a host of useful functions on campus, there are costs to consider, both financial and otherwise.

First, as Pilon and Bergquist (1979) point out, colleges are highly complex organizations: they often have unclear missions and goals and fragmented, semiautonomous programs. Faculty members tend to be wary and suspicious of "experts" outside of their disciplines, especially if these experts are associated with the college administration!

Second, despite the often decentralized control, college personnel can be highly sensitive to any suggestion that a consultant has paid insufficient attention to the college's "unique character." Consultants' recommendations must be handled with extreme care to forestall the dismissive accusation that "just because it works at South Central State doesn't mean that it will work here." The college administrator and others may spend so much time working through the politics of the consultation that they wonder whether the benefits were worth the effort involved.

Third, of course, is the financial cost. Hiring the right consultant can severely tax the institution's available budget, and at a time when discretionary funds may be increasingly difficult to locate. Further, as Pilon and Bergquist (1979) point out, consultant expenses may consume virtually all of the available resources, leaving little left over for on-campus support of the project, and—most critical—resources for follow-through.

Thus, the campus administrator is faced with a difficult trade-off (Matthews, 1983). What are the likely costs and benefits of engaging a consultant versus delegating the project internally? Here are some specific questions the administrator ought to ask:

> What, specifically, do I want a consultant to do that my own staff cannot do? What evidence is leading me to that conclusion?
>
> What would have to happen that would enable my staff to handle the problem or issue themselves?
>
> If the need is primarily for a particular *expertise,* could the need be met and costs reduced by sending staff to programs or workshops off campus?
>
> If the need is for problem definition or conflict resolution, how might campus resources be mobilized to address the issue?
>
> Assuming that a need for a truly external perspective exists, what are some alternative ways of gaining that perspective, short of hiring a consultant for one or more campus visits?

In the next chapter, Garth and Rehnke list several low-cost strategies for gaining assistance through informal networks. One of these strategies may be just the ticket, thus saving scarce resources for the subsequent interventions that may be needed.

I do not mean to suggest from all of these cautions that formal consultancies are unnecessary. Frequently they *are* necessary: local or more informal alternatives may be inadequate. However, the reader should reflect on how often consultants have been hired at significant institutional expense only to leave behind a set of recommendations on which no meaningful action is taken, for reasons economic, political, or both. (See Robert Toft's chapter on creating meaningful change in this volume for more information.)

Conclusion

Consultants alone are not the solution, but they can be the *beginning* of a solution. In a sense, of course, deciding whether or not to hire a consultant is interwoven with decisions regarding what *kind* of consultant to retain and whom to select. As Holtz (1989) points out, the administrator may not know if she needs a consultant until she finds out who might be available to help and what they can do. These are the topics addressed in the next two chapters.

References

Holtz, H. *Choosing and Using a Consultant: A Manager's Guide to Consulting Services.* New York: Wiley, 1989.

Matthews, J. B. *The Effective Use of Management Consultants in Higher Education.* Boulder, Colo.: National Center for Higher Education Management Systems, 1983.

Pilon, D. H., and Bergquist, W. H. *Consultation in Higher Education: A Handbook for Practitioners and Clients.* Washington, D.C.: Council of Independent Colleges, 1979.

Schein, E. H. *Process Consultation: Its Role in Organization Development.* Reading, Mass.: Addison-Wesley, 1969.

Schein, E. H. *Process Consultation.* Vol. 2: *Lessons for Managers and Consultants.* Reading, Mass.: Addison-Wesley, 1987.

Wergin, J. F. *Consulting in Higher Education: Principles for Institutions and Consultants.* Washington, D.C.: Association of American Colleges, 1989.

Jon F. Wergin is director of the Center for Educational Development and Faculty Resources at Virginia Commonwealth University in Richmond.

Several avenues are available for finding campus consultants.
Informal networking is becoming increasingly popular.

Variations on a Theme:
Colleague Consultant Networks

Russell Garth, Mary Ann Rehnke

The prior chapters consider the range and types of advice and assistance needed. We now want to address ways to find that advice.

Over the years, consulting networks based in national educational associations have provided such advice for campuses; the Association of American Colleges (AAC), the Council for the Advancement and Support of Education (CASE), and the Council of Independent Colleges (CIC) all have offered such networks as a service to their members. A network of consultants on a variety of subjects may have been created, or the consultants may be specialists on a specific area, such as technology and the liberal arts, as a result of their work with the association on a project.

The need for consultants can vary by type of institution. To provide concrete examples, we shall draw on our work with the Council of Independent Colleges, a national association of approximately three hundred private liberal arts colleges, which has had considerable experience in assisting its member institutions find consultants. In this group of institutions, the need for outside advice stems from two principal sources: the need for technical expertise and the fact that these colleges are often quite dynamic institutions.

1. *Need for technical expertise.* Many independent colleges without large endowments do not have available to them the same level of financial resources that many larger or public institutions do. Thus these colleges are not always able to hire as part of their permanent staff the kinds of technical expertise needed in a number of areas.

2. *Dynamic institutions.* Many independent colleges are often quite dynamic institutions. As colleges whose most basic mission is teaching

NEW DIRECTIONS FOR HIGHER EDUCATION, no. 73, Spring 1991 © Jossey-Bass Inc., Publishers

and as tuition-driven institutions, they are responsive to changing student interests and needs. As independent and typically small colleges, they have the organizational flexibility to design appropriate responses in a timely way. For example, during the past fifteen years, student curricular choices have undergone significant evolution, and independent colleges have often led the way in developing programs to respond to these needs. They have needed consultants to help them move into new areas.

Accordingly, CIC's national office has seen providing consultants and helping colleges to find consultants as an ongoing responsibility. This chapter catches us at an interesting time, however, since we are in an evolutionary process of gearing this help to a climate that seems to have changed in some basic ways.

Principle of Mutual Self-Help and the National Consulting Network

One of CIC's central tenets since its founding in 1956 has been mutual and cooperative self-help. In the mid 1950s, a group of fifty small, independent colleges were excluded—because they were unaccredited—from a major Ford Foundation grant to six hundred private colleges. The fifty unaccredited colleges banded together to form CIC's predecessor, the Council for the Advancement of Small Colleges. They reasoned that they could help each other achieve accreditation. They succeeded in that task in a few years but found that they had much to gain from continued cooperative effort and turned their ad hoc organization into a permanent association.

Indeed, through the years self-help, the cornerstone of the association, has gained an even greater intensity, since the center of gravity in higher education has shifted to large, public institutions. Smaller institutions have often discovered that they have to be increasingly vigilant about the kinds of advice and assistance they receive, since their needs and circumstances are sufficiently different from those of the larger, often research-focused institutions.

The principle of mutual self-help eventually led, in the mid 1970s, to CIC's development of the National Consulting Network for Liberal Arts Colleges. An early booklet introducing the network stated straightforwardly the rationale for this new program: "In spite of the abundance of consultants and consulting firms, administrators of small private colleges continue to have difficulty locating knowledgeable consultants who are familiar with the special needs of small colleges. . . . Experienced faculty and administrators from [CIC] colleges not only provide consulting services to member institutions but also are given opportunities to develop professionally through consulting experiences" (Council of Independent Colleges, n.d., p. 1).

The network included lists of potential consultants, organized in an elaborate taxonomy. These individuals were usually from small private colleges. If not, they were certainly individuals with experience in working with such colleges. In both cases, the individuals had agreed to work through the network for a modest, uniform honorarium instead of their usual consulting fees.

When colleges sought assistance through the network, CIC staff discussed needs with the college, identified several possible consultants and their availability for final selection by the college, served as an intermediary for the payment of fees, and made sure that evaluations of the experience by both parties took place.

This has been a clearly successful program. A large number of colleges have taken advantage of the service, and the feedback from both institutions and consultants has been highly positive. In recent years, however, use of the service has declined.

Consulting networks at other associations appear to be encountering the same trend. AAC, which started a structurally similar though more narrowly focused consulting network about five years later, has experienced similar declines in its use. CASE launched a similar service a few years ago and has also experienced declines in use by smaller independent colleges, despite increases by other types of institutions.

There appear to be several reasons for this decline in use at CIC. One of the most obvious is the more limited availability of grant monies to be spent on consultants. During the wave of reform in higher education during the 1970s, private foundations and federal government programs such as the Office of Education's Strengthening Developing Institutions Program (Title III of the Higher Education Act) encouraged the use of consultants for program development and evaluation and provided financial support for those purposes.

As a part of this general type of support, CIC was able to secure funds to staff the National Consulting Network and to publicize the program. The constant identification of consultants and need to learn the particulars of individual campuses made this program quite labor intensive. But the decreased availability of grants for consultant activities also affected CIC's central coordinating mechanism.

One result of these efforts was the creation of a cadre of consultants with expertise in a variety of areas. Colleges no longer had to rely on CIC to help them discover a scarce resource. Consultants were available and marketed themselves. As they developed competence and visibility in these areas, they became professional consultants who could command higher fees. This became an additional reason for the less frequent use of the consulting network and of consultants.

Colleague Consultants

Even though use of some association-based consulting networks has declined, the need for technical expertise on campuses has certainly not disappeared. Instead, campuses are turning to new means to acquire the expertise they need to tackle a problem or start a new program. One new trend is to rely on a more informal, ad hoc consultation through a respected colleague—the *colleague consultant.*

Colleague consultants play a significant role for many campus administrators, especially on the smaller campuses. A colleague consultant is a peer on a similar campus who can be contacted by letter, telephone, or facsimile machine to get advice on a problem, new program, or proposed policy. This type of consultant does *not* usually come to the caller's campus to analyze the situation and give advice. Rather, she responds based on her experience on her own campus, describing how the program, policy, or problem was addressed there. Because peers share similar perspectives and responsibilities, they can more readily discuss how best to address the situation, based on the colleague consultant's experience.

Why is this type of advice helpful? First, many campus administrators are isolated by virtue of their profession; they may carry the title of director of counseling on their campus, implying that they head a staff of counselors with whom they may confer, but they may be the only professional counselor on a small campus. Still other administrators are isolated because they are the only person, no matter how large the campus, who has their type of responsibilities; for example, the president, academic vice-president, or dean of students does not have a peer on her campus with the same responsibilities and expertise. Other administrators on rural campuses may not have ready access to someone in a similar position just across town. Thus, geographical isolation or being the only administrator in that position makes it impossible to discuss a proposed change with a knowledgeable campus colleague. It is helpful to turn to a peer on another campus for advice.

A second reason for relying on a colleague consultant is that they have relevant experience; there is no point in completely reinventing the wheel, and most campus administrators cannot afford to take the time to do so. No one on your campus may have the appropriate experience, but usually no matter what policy, program, or problem is being addressed, someone somewhere has faced that situation before.

Third, the dollars are right. Colleague advice, though inexpensive, can save you from expensive mistakes costing money and staff time. Most colleagues are flattered to be asked for their advice, as long as it requires a minimum amount of time, and are willing to send you their program or policy to use as a model as you develop your own. The only cost becomes that of the telephone call, letter, or facsimile.

With these good reasons for using a colleague consultant, how do you go about finding colleagues with the appropriate expertise? There are a number of obvious avenues. Most of those are worth pursuing.

Conferences. There are, of course, standard approaches such as attending conferences. We have all had experiences of learning more at a conference over coffee with a colleague than in a conference session. Indeed, CIC does what it can at conferences to promote such conversations by building informal networking opportunities into the conference—through continental breakfasts each morning, organized Dutch treat dinners, a mentor program for new deans, a luncheon for women administrators, breakfast for black college deans, receptions, and an opening banquet. Most associations do the same.

If administrators find themselves at conferences without such opportunities, they can create them for themselves. Ask speakers who are addressing a topic that concerns your campus to share a cup of coffee or breakfast with you. Get their names and telephone numbers and give them a call after the conference. Talk to new colleagues at the coffee break or call colleagues whom you know prior to the conference and arrange to have lunch with them.

Referrals. CIC, like many associations, accumulates information about the various activities of its member institutions and is happy to share it. Many associations also take additional steps, as does CIC, to enhance the ability to point individuals in the right direction. For example, in addition to reading college magazines, press releases, and newspapers, CIC also conducts annual surveys of college presidents and deans asking about their distinctive programs. In addition, CIC has visited over two hundred campuses in the past several years and conducts a variety of special projects and workshops that reveal interesting practices.

The point is that there is a great deal of experience among colleagues that can provide needed advice and that some existing connections, such as association activities and brokering, can be inexpensive ways to develop your own ideas.

Flexible Networks

Based on the increasing use of colleagues serving as informal consultants for each other, CIC has also begun to experiment with some more focused and loosely organized networking activities to enable administrators of independent colleges to find such advice when they need it. These activities are still in the early stages of development, but they seem worth describing now since they may be provocative for other collections of institutions to begin working on.

Such flexible networks with CIC should have several characteristics. First, they should build on the CIC principles of cooperative self-help and colleague consultants. Second, they should operate largely without CIC's national office as a constant facilitator. This probably means having some printed lists. Third, they should enable colleges to find advice precisely tailored for their needs.

Deans Advice Network. CIC is developing a Deans Advice Network. Academic vice-presidents, who often also carry the title of dean on the private college campus, who register for the annual Deans Institute are asked to list a few areas in which they have experience; examples would be faculty development, program review, and revising the faculty handbook. A topical directory indicating the various areas in which the deans have experience is created, and the deans' names are listed by the areas in which they have expertise. A second part of the directory lists deans in alphabetical order with addresses, telephone numbers, and all the areas in which each dean has experience. Sometimes knowing that a colleague has dealt with several areas, rather than just one, may prove helpful. The directory is revised each year prior to the Deans Institute, and each participant is given a copy.

State Networks. Another way of finding colleague consultants is through state meetings. In many states the presidents or the academic vice-presidents gather for a semiannual meeting to compare notes and hear a speaker discuss a current issue or address common concerns. At these meetings, administrators get to know one another and learn on whom they may call to discuss a variety of issues. These meetings are often very inexpensive because they can occur on a college campus and can often be conducted in just one day, given the geography of most states. State association staffs can be helpful in organizing such meetings, or two administrators holding the same title at different campuses can invite their colleagues to gather. These low-cost meetings are a simple means of finding peers to call on to discuss an issue.

Based on an informal survey of private colleges, the following states currently have a meeting for private college chief academic affairs officers: Arkansas, Iowa, Kansas, Kentucky, Minnesota, Missouri, Nebraska, New Jersey, North Carolina, South Carolina, Tennessee, Virginia, West Virginia, and Wisconsin. Deans in other states such as Connecticut have expressed interest in founding associations, so more state meetings may appear.

Program Review. One of the chief uses of CIC's National Consulting Network has been finding individuals who could evaluate and advise individual departments or programs. CIC is presently developing a network for this purpose that would rely on mutual relationships between chief academic officers. CIC has asked academic deans to provide names of administrators or faculty on their campuses who would be able to review programs on other campuses. CIC intends to publish this list, with some recommended guidelines on fees and other costs, so that deans can make such arrangements directly with other deans. Perhaps some mutual exchanges would even emerge.

Planned Visits. It is possible to capitalize in a focused way on relationships with colleagues. One private college president just visited six similar institutions, whose presidents he knew well. Spending approximately two days at each campus, he sought answers to questions that his administrators had given him before he left, talked privately with each president, and in one case met with the board of trustees. In each case, the visit seemed to offer mutual benefit made possible by the shared commitments understood through prior relationships. We also know of other versions, such as reciprocal visits of administrative teams.

State meetings for deans, informal networking at conferences, directories of expertise, and purposeful visits are all ways to find knowledgeable colleagues. These colleague consultants provide experience that most often is appropriate for your campus, is low-cost, takes little time from the consultant or the person asking the advice, and can save campuses time in facing a new situation. In many cases, an external, paid independent consultant is needed, but many administrators will also be well served in other situations by having a wider repertoire of ways to get advice.

Reference

Council of Independent Colleges. *National Consulting Network for Liberal Arts Colleges.* Washington, D.C.: Council of Independent Colleges, n.d.

Russell Garth is vice-president of the Council of Independent Colleges. He was previously program officer and deputy director of the Fund for the Improvement of Postsecondary Education.

Mary Ann Rehnke is director of annual programs at the Council of Independent Colleges and has served as associate dean at the College of Saint Catherine, St. Paul, Minnesota, and Daemen College, Amherst, New York.

There are steps the client can take to reduce the risk of choosing the wrong consultant.

Finding the Right Consultant

George Dehne

You know you need a consultant. That's a good start. But how do you find the right consultant to solve your institution's problem effectively and without causing hysteria throughout the college? It is a good question and a difficult one to answer.

Anyone can be a consultant. You do not have to pass an examination or, in most cases, have a license. Advertise that you are a consultant, and suddenly you are one. To gain an aura of credibility, consultants in some fields can join trade associations that require members to uphold certain ethical standards and play by certain rules. In higher education, these groups are few and far between. Additionally, virtually any consultant can join these groups. Membership simply demonstrates good intent, not necessarily competence.

Unfortunately, there is also a societal belief that most consultants are people who were fired and could not find another job. I say unfortunately because this image casts a shadow over the consulting business. The "loser turned rip-off" image makes selecting the right consultant even more difficult. You have to find not only competence but also someone who instills trust. Lack of any credentialing process makes choosing the right consultant difficult.

Because anyone can tout himself or herself as a consultant, many people do so. As Daniel Pilon pointed out in Chapter One, there are many consultants in higher education. There are "spontaneous" consultants, men and women with jobs on a college campus who are asked by another college for advice—at a price. Once touched by the consultant bug, many of these people actively solicit business, and they are sometimes very good consultants.

Executives at many institutions have formal agreements with their institutions for release time to consult. In many ways, reaccreditation visiting team members are consultants.

A final group consists of the full-time consultants and consulting firms. These too crop up like weeds in spring. At last count there were about fifteen firms that claim to be market research experts in student recruitment, not including the hundreds of corporate market research firms that occasionally do work for colleges. The number of consultants available is staggering. Finding the right one is the difficulty.

Due to ease of access into the business and sheer numbers, variety is also a contributing factor in making the consultant selection process complicated. A consultant is available for virtually any problem. In fund-raising alone there are capital campaigns, annual funds, deferred giving, management, research, major gifts, direct mail, and telethon consultants, and everything in between. In these and other cases, a firm with a specialty in one area also may claim or have expertise in another area. Sorting out the various strengths of consultants who might help your institution can be difficult.

Despite the number and variety, it can still be difficult to find even the names of consultants. There is no directory of higher education consultants. The ideal person for your consulting task may be on the campus ten miles away, but without some digging you may never know it. Then again, you may be bombarded by mail and calls from consulting firms with track records in your area of concern.

Earlier in this book you read about networking to obtain the names of appropriate consultants. The advice given there should help you get through the web and, at least, help you find names of possible consultants. But what do you do next? Identifying the "right" consultant is critical, and there is no neat and easy process to follow. However, here are some steps you can take to reduce the risk of the dreaded "consult bungle."

Step One: Know What You Wish to Accomplish

Step one in finding the right consultant is knowing what you wish to accomplish. This advice might seem obvious, but following through on it is not always easy. With multiple needs and concerns, institutions have difficulty limiting expectations on the one hand and identifying the "real" issue on the other. For example, is getting more income from your bookstore a management, buying, or space issue? An environmental consultant will tell you it is a space issue, while a marketing consultant may tell you it is a management problem. If you cannot identify the problem, then the ideal consultant is a generalist—perhaps the director of a similar bookstore at another college. This person can access the problem for and with you. Once the problem is identified, the specialist consultant can be called in.

Your institution's personnel should outline the desired outcomes of a consultancy, describe the expected procedures, and determine the price they are willing to pay to get the advice. This becomes a guideline for selecting a consultant. A request for proposal (RFP), which is standard among state-supported institutions, can play an important role in helping an institution clarify its goals. The RFP, however, does not need to be bureaucratic and difficult to understand. It should be straightforward and simple.

Who Should Determine the Need? You must expect to take some time analyzing the need. To get the most for the money and to gain acceptance for the consultant, the affected constituencies should be involved. Three approaches—the task force approach, the community involvement approach, and the administrative approach—tend to be most effective.

The Task Force Approach. In this case, key players determine the need and desired outcome. The task force should include a representative sample of constituencies.

The Community Involvement Approach. Polling a wide spectrum of the campus on the issue at hand characterizes this approach. For example, to assess needs concerning the library, ask students, faculty, and administrators to describe how they use the library, what would they like to see in a library, and what is wrong with the current library. This approach limits charges from certain quarters that they were not consulted, but it tends to raise expectations.

The Administrative Approach. The least political of the approaches, the administrative approach simply puts the assessment of the needs in the hands of those who have to manage and budget the area in question. However, the administrator should check informally with others who might be affected by a consultation.

Writing the Request for Proposal. Keep the RFP simple. First, describe the situation in some detail. Explain what the suspected problem is and why action is being taken at this time. Indicate the possible causes for the problem and the alternative solutions already discussed. For example, if the library is the issue, explain whether or not a new library is a real possibility. If it is not, make sure the consultant knows. List what changes are possible (for example, renovation, expansion of existing library, change of buildings).

Second, list the questions you want answered by the consultant. Be as specific as possible. "What should we do with our library?" is not an effective question. Instead ask, "How do we get more study space for students? Can we find room for faculty research? Can we rearrange stacks for better access to our most often used collections? Would renovation of the library provide more effective space?"

Third, list the kinds of steps you have in mind and a rough time line. If interviewing or surveying is involved, let the consultant know those are acceptable options. A time line is especially important. A busy consultant does not want to bid on something that he or she cannot possibly deliver.

Fourth, list the price you are willing to pay for the service. I recommend including in the RFP the maximum dollar amount allotted for the project. Most colleges guard this information because they think a consultant will immediately charge the budgeted amount. This may happen, but at least there will be no surprises. Most consultants want to help you. If they know your budget, they will either develop a proposal that meets your needs and falls within the budget or not offer a proposal. If no consultant chooses to make a proposal, you will know your estimate is too low. I have seen many institutions fall into disarray when proposals for services came in far higher than expected. An announced limit with some flexibility prevents "sticker shock" and provides the consultant with a chance to make a reasonable proposal. You can ask several consultants for an estimated price prior to writing the RFP.

Once the RFP is completed, ask several people who are not connected to the process to read it and reiterate what it says. If they do not understand the request, the consultant may not either.

Provide a contact person and a telephone number on your RFP. Invite consultants to call and ask questions. Even the best RFPs raise questions.

Evaluating the Proposals. Now that you have received the proposals, you have to evaluate each one. You should look for the following:

1. Is there an understanding of the issue? Is the consultant reiterating what you think you said, or is it different? A consultant may have misinterpreted the problem, or you may not have made it clear enough.

2. Are there references in the proposal to similar situations that the consultant handled? Experience is important.

3. Does the proposal discuss specific issues? A boilerplate proposal will talk generally, not specifically. A thoughtful proposal should address each issue raised in your proposal and explain how it will be handled. If there are alternative ways to approach the issue, the proposal should outline them and request a meeting for clarification. Be suspicious of a proposal that offers no alternatives. If each alternative has a different cost, they should all be listed.

4. Does the proposal address (not answer) all the questions you raised in your RFP? If a question is overlooked, call for confirmation that it is tacitly addressed or question the consultant during a presentation.

After answering these questions, evaluating the proposal may still be difficult. There will be similarities among the approaches. However, the top candidates should have responded directly to the request for proposal, not have prepared a generic checklist.

Step Two: Know What Results to Expect

Expecting too much from a consultant can be frustrating. Generally, a consultant brings one or more of the following dimensions to your interaction. Determining which is most important to your institution is essential in the hiring decision.

Providing an Impartial Opinion. Robert Townsend wrote in *Up the Organization* (1970, p. 104), "They [consultants] are the people who borrow your watch then tell you what time it is." There is truth in this. Too often organizations do not take time to look at their watch, or the crystal is dirty, or the watch may not be set correctly. A consultant can look at the watch with a critical eye, set the time, if necessary, or simply agree that it works fine.

Interpreting Information and Data. Many colleges collect volumes of information and data, only to find that the on-campus staff cannot interpret data into useful action steps, or they cannot agree on the meaning of the data. A consultant, comfortable with quantitative or qualitative information, can provide valuable insight into the meaning of the numbers and suggest ways to utilize what is discovered.

Bringing News from the Outside. Anyone who has spent time at one institution knows that it is difficult to gain a perspective on other colleges. An experienced consultant who has worked with colleges similar to yours can provide a more accurate assessment of your institution's strengths, weaknesses, distinctions, practices, and so forth. Many consultants can offer tips on activities that he or she knows work because they have been successful elsewhere.

Offering Creative Solutions. Consultants have the time to focus on a problem and develop a solution. They are not concerned about the day-to-day administrative issues or politics. Blend this freedom to attack the problem with some creativity and experience, and a consultant should be able to provide innovative solutions.

Admittedly, many colleges may have enough creativity on campus to recommend solutions to marketing problems. However, creativity per se is not the issue. It is the luxury of time to explore the options fully that eludes the frantic (albeit creative) administrator.

Gaining Credibility for an Activity. "There are no prophets in one's native land" goes an old adage. This also explains another need for consultants. Often a staff member or an entire staff recognizes the need to change directions, yet trustees, faculty, or administrators are reluctant to move. A consultant can be the militia. He or she can ride in, listen to the staff members, and declare that this or that should be done. Armed with assumed greater knowledge, even the most recalcitrant resistance will usually back off. Admittedly, it would be a simpler world if we could appreciate the judgments of those on the staff, but "the grass is always greener on the other side of the fence."

Some consultants can offer all of these services, but be sure you know which are most important to you. Your line of questioning and your RFP should concentrate on the key items.

Part-Time Campus-Based Consultant Versus Full-Time For-Profit Consultant. Most likely, regardless of the situation, you will have the choice of an employee at another college who consults or a full-time consultant who specializes in the area of concern. Even cost differences do not help the decision making here. A campus-based consultant who is in demand may charge a higher fee than a full-time consultant.

Part-time and full-time consultants have somewhat different strengths. On-campus consultants usually are more familiar with the day-to-day problems of the business. These people know how their operation works and how yours compares to theirs. They are usually advocates for the on-campus staff and generally less critical than full-time consultants. Since they know the problems, they do not raise expectations. However, they may have limited exposure to other colleges.

Full-time consultants are out of the day-to-day work. They may be out of touch with the operation end. However, depending on experience, full-time consultants should bring more current "news from the outside" and have a greater appreciation of what works elsewhere.

Step Three: Identifying Possible Consultants

Unfortunately, there is no single source that will lead an institution to the various consultants who can meet its needs. Identifying possible consultants is an art in itself. In the previous chapter on networking, you learned how to use your contacts to identify consultants. Here I will mention only in passing where to find consultants.

Higher Education Associations. The associations in Washington and elsewhere often maintain lists of consultants. Most associations will provide names but not make recommendations. Often the program director, the person who sets up workshops and the annual conference, is the best to call. He or she is always looking for good speakers. Some organizations such as the Council for the Advancement and Support of Education (CASE) have "associate" members (usually consultants) listed in their directories.

Networking Through Colleagues. Call your friends at other colleges or call similar institutions for names of consultants. Ideally, you will know of an institution with a similar problem. If they used a consultant, they will still have the name.

Step Four: Choose a Consultant with Expertise in Primary Area of Concern

Management consultant Peter Drucker (1980) talks about hiring people for the heart of the job: that is, identify a person with strength in the most important aspect of the job description. Do not hire a person for her or his peripheral strengths if she or he is not the best person to do the heart of the job.

Colleges tend *not* to hire for the heart of the job. Financial situations often lure us into thinking we can stretch a person's talent and get more for the money. Just look at a typical public relations office. There is usually some writer who also serves as a photographer or vice versa. But what is the person's most important job: writing or photography?

The same holds true of consultants. An expert in annual funds is not necessarily the person to hire for a capital campaign. Consultants, like many colleges, want to be all things to all people. However, most consultants have made their mark in one way or another. Find out what each consultant's strengths and experience are and if they match the needs of your institution. The following are some things to look for.

Read the Background Sheet or Vitae. Every consultant should be able to supply background data. Review the kinds of jobs he or she held in higher education, if any. Do they relate to the area where you seek help? For example, a publications director does not necessarily know market research or media relations. How long was the consultant at a particular job? Is there any indication of success? Is there variety in the jobs held? The same job at similar institutions may be fine if you are also that kind of institution.

Review the Client List. An amplified client list can tell you volumes. Request a client list that includes services rendered. A one-day workshop offered at X college can be on a client list, but it should be stated as such. In your request for proposal ask the consultant to describe the services performed for the clients listed. Additionally, it is wise to ask for dates of the services, names of contact persons, and the contacts' telephone numbers. (It may be difficult to find a reference at an organization where work was done more than three years ago.) Look for institutions that have used similar services. Determine the kind of service the consultant provides most often and determine if it matches what your institution seeks.

Does the consultant work with institutions similar to yours or with quite different kinds of colleges? This can be a major question, depending on the service the consultant offers. For example, assessing a public relations operation at a small college requires someone who understands the resource limitations of a small college. However, you also must consider what part of the industry is the most innovative and futuristic. If you are seeking state-of-the-art strategies for marketing a public institution, then a consultant with experience at private colleges might be best. Private colleges, out of necessity, have led the way in effective recruitment programs.

Does the consultant have the greatest experience inside or outside higher education? This too is an issue that depends on the area in question. Consultants with experience in business can often shed new light on certain issues. They tend to be more decisive about personnel issues. Additionally, they are not hindered by history.

However, higher education is a highly politicized and esoteric field.

Consultants in higher education tend to be more sensitive to the views of faculty and the "ethics" of higher education. Also, you are less likely to "rediscover the wheel" when using a consultant who has a great deal of experience in higher education.

Choose a consultant with experience in higher education if you are seeking a consultation in an area that may affect the faculty or are not in a position to take risks.

Check References. Two factors make getting credible information on a reference check more difficult than you might expect. First, no one likes being wrong. Who wants to admit they wasted several thousand dollars on a consultant? You will generally get evasive rather than negative responses from a client who was not satisfied. Additionally, the contact may have befriended the consultant. After talking to the contact listed by the consultant, ask for someone else at the college who is familiar with that consultant's work, or talk to someone at your institution who has a contact at the other college.

Second, the contact's college may have received the service they wanted, but it may not be the service you seek. Make sure you are comparing apples to apples. For example, the contact may have been looking for a consultant who would add credibility to an activity already under discussion while you are seeking an innovative solution to a problem.

To get the most out of a reference, ask the following questions:

1. Were you the primary contact with the consultant? If not, who was?
2. Please describe what you were seeking when you retained the consultant. (Make sure the outcome matches what you seek from the consulting experience.)
3. Can you describe what the consultant contributed to your institution? (Listen to make sure that the description parallels your expectations.)
4. How well did the consultant interact with other administrators, faculty, students, and so forth? (If there was little interaction, the consultant may have a pro forma approach. Also listen for comments about difficulties with one group or another.)
5. Did the person who made the presentation or wrote the proposal head the team? (Be wary of absentee senior consultants. The "bait and switch" is fairly common.)
6. Were the results tailored to your institution's needs and delivered on time?
7. On a scale of one to ten, with ten being very satisfied, where would you rank your experience with the consultant? (Any rating below six should be suspect.)
8. Would you hire the consultant again? If not, why not?
9. Did you consider any other consultants? If so, who? Why did you decide not to use them?

Step Five: The Presentation

One of the best consultants in a particular area may be incompatible with your institution's ethos. Trust and comfort as well as a consultant's proven expertise are essential to a good consulting relationship. The presentation can help you evaluate the match between a consultant and your institution. (If it is a low-budget, low-risk consultancy, then a presentation may not be necessary. Many consultants will not make a presentation if the contract will be under $10,000. In these cases, reference checks and proposal evaluation will have to suffice.)

The Arrangements. Ask for presentations after the consultants have reviewed the RFP but before a proposal has been made. Without an RFP, the consultant will not know if he or she can meet your needs. Of course, the opposite is also true: you and your group will not know which consultant can answer your questions. Additionally, the consultant should be able to use what is learned in the meeting to develop a specific and unique proposal for your institution.

Leave plenty of time for each presenter. Consultants may travel several hours to reach your institution, so you should provide at least two to three hours for each presentation. Most consultants will not use this much time, but an engaging discussion could.

Make sure all those involved in the selection are present. Also remember that the first presenter has a disadvantage. You will learn from the first visit and become better interviewers as time passes. Call the first presenter after the presentations if you feel you did not learn enough about his or her capabilities.

What to Look and Listen For. Consultants must be good listeners. Watch the presenter. Does he or she listen to questions as they relate to your situation, or is the presentation "canned"? Is the presenter familiar with the RFP and your institution? Can the presenter speak for the organization? A slick presenter may be simply a salesperson. He or she may not be authorized to quote a price or offer a proposed schedule. Does the consultant have questions? No questions usually means the consultant is offering a standard package.

Is the consultant offering a didactic solution or a fluid one? Many consultants feel there is only one way to solve a specific problem, while others are willing to offer options and alternatives. If you want direction, then the didactic approach is fine. If you want to be a teammate with the consultant, then you will be more comfortable with the fluid approach.

How Should You Feel? This may seem like a strange question, but you should like and respect the presenter (if he or she is the consultant). Personal incompatibility can destroy a consultancy. A college with a relaxed atmosphere will be incompatible with a formal consultant, and vice versa. The personal style of the consultant should reflect the self-image of the institution. While confidence in the consultant should be the foremost criterion, compatibility should not be far behind.

Step Six: Be Flexible

There is no contradiction between having a clear sense of what you wish to accomplish and remaining flexible. Flexibility and changing objectives are two quite different animals. Because consultants represent a special expertise, it is not uncommon for a consultant to recommend adjusting an assumption or changing the scope of a project. Your willingness to make midcourse corrections can help ensure a successful relationship. A consultancy should be a dialogue with significant give-and-take. Even after you have received a proposal and chosen a consultant, be prepared for some adjustments. A proposal is just that: a putting forward of ideas for your consideration based on what is known at the time. If in the course of the discussion or the actual consultancy it becomes clear that the real issue is other than expected, you and the consultant must be willing to adjust. To ensure that a consultant can be flexible, ask for examples of changes made during a prior consultancy. If the consultant can provide no examples, then he or she probably believes in the "one solution fits all" approach.

Conclusion

There are no guarantees that the consultant you choose will be the best for your institution. All you can do is follow some of the recommendations in this chapter. A combination of common sense and intuition also will help. The time you spend finding the right consultant is far less costly than choosing a consultant who disrupts the institution, irritates key constituencies, and wastes money.

References

Drucker, P. F. *Managing in Turbulent Times.* New York: Harper & Row, 1980.
Townsend, R. *Up the Organization: How to Stop the Corporation from Stifling People and Strangling Profits.* New York: Knopf, 1970.

George Dehne, a higher education consultant based in New York, has worked with more than fifty colleges to create strategies to improve admissions, financial aid, and public relations programs.

*Once the consultant has been chosen, details may need negotiation, and
a contract protecting both parties must be drawn up and signed.*

Negotiating the Contract

Lynn Curry

To this point the contractor and the consultant have made initial contact
to identify preliminary fit between their interests, capabilities, experience,
and availability. The contractor has included the consultant in the short
list of likely consultants and communicated that degree of perceived fit to
the consultant by sending to the consultant the request for proposal (RFP).
The RFP has concisely communicated what is to be done, with what time
line, and with what resources. The consultant has submitted a proposal on
time that details an understanding of the contractor's needs, consultant's
approach, methodology and work plan, project staffing, time lines, fee
structure, and resource use. The contractor has met its end of the bargain
by adhering to the published timetable for consultant selection, a process
that may have included a personal presentation from the consultant.

The decision is finally made that a particular consultant should be
awarded the contract. The next steps are to confirm the contract details
regarding time, personnel costs, payout dates, and deliverable dates. This
negotiation is referred to as the "haggle." The agreement reached must be
captured in some form of contract between the contractor and the consultant. These two issues, the haggle and the contract, will be reviewed in this
chapter.

The Haggle

If the match between what the consultant has proposed in the RFP and
what you as the contractor want and can afford is perfect, there is no need
to haggle, and the parties should move directly to working up and signing a
contract. The negotiating haggle occurs only if the contractor wants the

consultant to do most or part but not all of the RFP prepared by that consultant. If this is the case, the contractor and the consultant must negotiate changes to the consultant's proposal. These changes will probably not be in the substantive sections of the RFP: the general objectives, consultant approach, and general methodology. More often the contractor has difficulty with some of the contract details, including the time lines or work plan, personnel assigned for project staff, cost of the project, payout dates, or delivery dates. These issues are usually reducible to dollars and profit margins. If the contractor wants the work done more quickly, with cheaper staff at a lower cost, with delayed payout dates or moved-up delivery dates, the consultant will quite reasonably reply, "You can get work done well, done quickly, or done cheaply, but you only get two out of three!"

In opening the negotiation haggle, the contractor should indicate clearly the areas of the basic proposal that are acceptable and the areas of remaining concern. Both parties must follow rules of good negotiation throughout this exchange and over the next period of time while both sides consult with colleagues, investigate options, and make further proposals. The principles of good negotiation have been detailed in a number of recent publications, including those by Keiser (1988, 1989) and Paton (1988).

One of the most straightforward of these is Fisher and Ury's *Getting to Yes: Negotiating Agreement Without Giving In* (1983). These authors outline an approach to negotiation that both is practical and follows common sense. Central to their approach is the instruction that neither side should mindlessly stick to its initial position as a way to avoid looking into the real issues. Both sides must come to understand the needs and the interests of the other in some detail and then proceed to investigate, generate, and propose alternate ideas that satisfy everyone's interests and needs.

The contractor must understand in detail what the consultant needs to adequately perform the work and to further the consultant's business. The consultant needs to understand the real interests of the contractor. What are the limitations in which the contractor must operate? What is the minimum the contractor needs to receive from the work, by what time, and for what reasons? The more straightforward each side can be with the other about these basic needs and concerns, the more quickly each side can move to proposing options for mutual gain.

Both sides must be creative. For example, if the total cost is a problem, some of the following options may provide a solution acceptable to both sides:

1. Extend the time line for the work to go beyond the close of one fiscal year. This will allow the contractor to pay out the same amount of money, but in two fiscal periods, which may be easier.

2. Recategorize the cost. Instead of charging for consultant days, consider some of these days "staff training." It may be easier for the contractor

to pay for staff training or for a mix of consultant days and staff training. The actual work of the consultant need not change.

3. Bill more days to lessen the per diem amount. If the problem is that the consultant per diem is greater than a suggested maximum, then bill the number of days necessary to cover the consultant's per diem. For example, if the work is projected at five days at $1,000 per day (total $5,000), but the limit is $500 per day, then bill for ten days of work at $500 per day (total $5,000).

4. Change the basis of payment. If the problem is the total personnel budget, consider converting the payment to some other format. For example, travel vouchers can be purchased for the consultant to use outside the project; books, subscriptions, and publications can be purchased for the consultant; computer or office equipment can be purchased for the consultant; and so forth.

Note that each of these creative solutions used will have to appear in the contract to be signed between the parties.

The consultant might be willing to renegotiate on all points, including the costs and profit margin, without any creative solution proposed by the contractor. Consultants often inflate their cost estimates to provide themselves with the maximum options for delivering the work, to inflate their profit margins, or to protect themselves from unknown price increases if the work plan covers several months. The contractor should be doing this haggle with the lead consultant, who should have a firm idea of exactly where the proposal is padded and how much negotiating room there is before the benefits of doing the contract disappear. Negotiations should take place only between parties who have both the information and the authority to negotiate and to make decisions.

It is important that both sides in the haggle know their BATNA (Best Alternative to Negotiated Agreement). This BATNA should be shared with the other side if the negotiations are not going well. The consultant must know at what point it becomes nonrewarding to complete the proposed work. The contractor must have made decisions about what it can do without and still get the main objective of the work. The BATNA for the contractor is not always getting a new consultant. The consultant with whom the contractor is haggling may be the best for the job by a wide margin, and still all the creative options may not work. In such a case, a contractor should consult with colleagues and superiors to develop a clear sense of what the best alternative will be if the negotiations with the consultant are unsuccessful. Often this means reconceptualizing the work to be done, perhaps staging the work to meet the available dollars. The BATNA for the consultant is often identical to that for the contractor, in which case they have discovered a mutually agreeable option.

The Contract

The central objective for a contract is to provide legal protection for both parties in the event of difficulties encountered during or at the conclusion of the project.

Goals. Six specific goals that should be accomplished with any contract signed by both contractor and consultant have been identified by Shenson (1990). The contract must

1. Avoid misunderstandings
2. Maintain working independence and freedom
3. Ensure work
4. Ensure payment
5. Avoid liability
6. Prevent litigation.

Avoid Misunderstandings. The contract must spell out what the consultant will do and by when. Depending on the type of contract chosen, this specification will be more or less detailed. A balance must be struck between providing too much detail and allowing an opportunity for misunderstanding between consultant and contractor. When in doubt, be specific.

Maintain Working Independence and Freedom. The consultant must be left free to conduct the work outlined in the proposal, or as detailed in the haggle, in a comfortable manner. If the contractor imposes an additional list of specifications at the contract stage, the consultant will feel that his or her freedom and independence have been infringed on and will resist accepting such a contract.

Ensure Work. The contract must ensure the consultant's award of the work and that the contractor will not cancel any part of that work during its course. The consultant at this point has obligated staff, resources, and time to the completion of the negotiated work. The contract is the consultant's protection that this investment will not be made in vain.

Ensure Payment. The contract must also assure that the consultant will be paid. It is not unusual for a contract to specify a down payment for the consultant prior to beginning any work on the negotiated project. This is particularly the case if the consultant has to carry significant up-front costs, such as extensive travel, hiring specialized personnel, or purchasing specialized equipment, to complete the work. The consultant should not be expected to "loan" the cost of these expenses to the contractor for the length of the project or even until the first deliverable date. In general, a specified amount for the down payment and subsequent amounts deliverable throughout the project, reserving no more than 10 percent of the total fee for the final project report, should be specified in the contract. Each payout should be specified by date or by a deliverable to be produced by the consultant.

Avoid Liability. The issue of consultant liability, if applicable, must be addressed in the contract. Depending on the project and the type of advice sought from the consultant, legal liability will be more or less a threat to the parties concerned. Both should consult legal advisers regarding the extent of potential liability and reflect this advice in their mutual contract.

Prevent Litigation. A complete contract should cover the possibility of litigation between the consultant and the client. Generally, litigation becomes a possibility only when the contractor feels the work has not been properly done or has not paid the consultant as specified. If possible, a contract should specify means of resolving these difficulties without recourse to the courts. Methods such as binding arbitration, third-party review, and use of an arbitration firm paid for equally by the parties may be useful to specify in the contract.

Types of Contract. There are many different types of contracts, which vary in terms of their formality and their ultimate weight in a court of law should litigation occur. There are five functional levels of formality in contracts: verbal agreements, letters of intent, one-page contracts, purchase orders or firm retainers, and specialized written contracts.

Verbal Agreements. Generally, contractors and consultants should avoid doing business on the basis of verbal agreements. Even for the most simple agreement between friends to do a very straightforward piece of work (for example, prepare a literature review for a certain price by a certain date), there are at least three different areas of potential misunderstanding: how extensive the review, for how much money, and by what date.

Letters of Intent. The minimal level of contracting should always be the informal letter contract (see Figure 1). This is a straightforward letter between the consultant and contractor. Either party could initiate the letter, but receipt and agreement must be confirmed and noted by both parties. This letter must include the following:

1. Name of the contractor and the consultant
2. Specification of what consultant services are being contracted for
3. Specification of the date those services will be supplied
4. Specification of the fee for the services supplied
5. Specification of how ancillary expenses (for example, travel, meals, accommodation) will be handled.

This level of contract is particularly appropriate for very short consultant engagements. Examples are one-session speeches, one- or two-day group facilitations, and reviews and critiques of single documents or proposals.

One-Page Contracts. One step up from the minimal informal letter is a letter accompanying a one-page contract (see Figure 2). This form of con-

Figure 1. Informal Letter Contract

Curry Adams
& Associates / Associés Inc.

Miss Marsha Sharp   September 11, 1990
Executive Director
Canadian Dietetic Association
480 University Avenue
Suite 601
Toronto, Ontario
M5G 1V2

Dear Miss Sharp:

Re: Consultation Services—October 1, 1990

This letter will serve as confirmation of the decision of the Canadian Dietetic Association to contract my services in the capacity of Consultant for the day of October 1, 1990.

My fee for service is $1,000 per day plus expenses for travel, meals and accommodation. In order to facilitate matters, all travel arrangements will be made by my office.

Enclosed is a worksheet to be used by Councils to prepare their presentations. We will need about 30 copies.

Cordially,

Lynn Curry, Ph.D.
Principal

cc   Sue Ross

#1015, 130 rue Albert Street, Ottawa, Ontario, Canada K1P 5G4   Tel: (613) 567-0622 Fax: (613) 567-0623

Figure 2. One-Page Contract

Curry Adams
& Associates / Associés Inc.

Brenda Myers   November 13, 1989
Executive Director
Canadian Physiotherapy Association
890 Yonge Street
9th Floor
Toronto, Ontario

Dear Brenda:

Included with this note will be a draft version of a "contract letter" between the Canadian Physiotherapy Association and Curry Adams & Associates, Inc. I constructed this letter based on our notes following our meeting October 30, 1989.

Please make whatever changes better suit you and return two signed copies, one of which I will countersign and return to you. Alternatively, if this letter is acceptable as is, please make a photocopy and return one signed copy to me.

Since our meeting I have had a couple of sessions with Doug Angus, and we have begun data collection on his section of the work. That included, as you will recall, a restaurant review guide to fine dining in Ottawa!

Cordially,

Lynn Curry

Encl.

#1015, 130 rue Albert Street, Ottawa, Ontario, Canada K1P 5G4   Tel: (613) 567-0622   Fax: (613) 567-0623

Figure 2. (*continued*)

Curry Adams
& Associates / Associés Inc.

October 30, 1989

—CONTRACT—

Following our meeting of this date, the undersigned undertake on behalf of their organizations a contract for stages 1, 2, 3, 4 as outlined in the proposal presented to the Canadian Physiotherapy Association, September 12, 1989. Dollar amounts for consultant time follow the outline for stages 1 through 4 as in the proposal; travel/accommodation cost will be reimbursed on a receipt basis. Invoices will be submitted as each major task is completed. Total invoiced amounts will never exceed the amounts projected in the proposal.

Work plan time lines call for stage 1 to be completed and invoiced before December 8, 1989. Work on stage 2 will be conducted between February 1, 1990 and May 1, 1990; stage 3 work will begin in November, 1989 and will conclude at the end of February, 1990. Stage 4 work will begin in February, 1990 and conclude by May 1, 1990. Drafts of all reports (stage 2, 3, 4) will be filed with Brenda Myers on or before May 14, 1990 with final revisions completed by May 31, 1990.

The undersigned accept termination conditions for this contract to be nonacceptable performance on the part of either party which would abrogate the contract at any time.

The consultant undertakes to personally complete all outlined project tasks with the exception of the stage 3 trend analysis based on available data and literature to be completed by Doug Angus as outlined in the project proposal.

_____   _____

Lynn Curry   Brenda Myers
Curry Adams & Associates, Inc.   Canadian Physiotherapy Association

#1015, 130 rue Albert Street, Ottawa, Ontario, Canada K1P 5G4   Tel: (613) 567-0622 Fax: (613) 567-0623

tract has two sections: a letter outlining the intent between the contractor and consultant and a contract section. Either the consultant or the contractor can initiate these one-page contracts, but both must sign them prior beginning to any work. The contract section must specify by name the contractor and the consultant, a brief description of the work to be undertaken, the dates for work completion, the method of submitting the work, the dollar amounts to be paid out, the dates for those payments, and the method of payment. The one-page contract should also have a clause outlining termination conditions for either party. Other clauses to satisfy specific concerns of the consultant or the contractor may be necessary. In Figure 2, the contractor was concerned about the staffing for various sections of the work plan.

Retainers. The firm retainer form or purchase order (see Exhibit 1) has built in legal force due to its construction and the explicit provisions of the agreement that always accompanies the basic form. These purchase orders or firm retainer forms are always signed by the consultant and by the contractor and often include a signature from the business officer for the contractor. The forms specify the beginning and ending dates for the purchased services, the fee for those services on a daily, monthly, or yearly basis, and a brief outline of the services to be provided. The provisions that accompany this type of form, usually in small print on the back, also provide termination specifications, liability protection for the contractor, confidentiality restrictions on the consultant, and other elements of a complete written contract.

Specialized Written Contracts. The formal written contract should be drawn up by legal counsel to both parties. These contracts will always contain at least the following sections:

1. Definition of the signing parties, including legal addresses.
2. Date of agreement signing.
3. Indication that the contractor is seeking specific services and that the consultant is providing those specific services.
4. Explicit description of the services to be provided and purchased.
5. Explicit definition of the time of performance of services.
6. Details of the compensation to be paid to the consultant by the contractor. This should include the timing of compensation, for example, following a specified schedule, in response to an invoice from the consultant, on the basis of a fixed figure or formula, or on completion of specified services or portions of services.
7. A series of clauses protecting the consultant. These would include some or all of the following:
   a. Indication that the consultant is an independent contractor and not to be bound by the rules and regulations governing the contractor.

Exhibit 1. Retainer

Provisions of This Agreement

WHEREAS the University is desirous of obtaining the services of the Firm for the purpose of performing the Services,

AND WHEREAS the Firm is desirous of performing the Services for the University on the terms and conditions herein set out,

WITNESSETH that in consideration of the premises and covenants herein, the parties agree as follows:

1. Definitions

   In this Agreement, the following expressions have the following meanings:

   a. "Agreement" means this agreement between the University and the Firm, including the provisions on the reverse side hereof.
   b. "Designated Contact" means the qualified and competent individual or individuals designated by the Firm and approved by the University, which may act arbitrarily in giving such approval, and being an employee of the Firm.
   c. "Fee" means the fee referred to on the reverse side hereof.
   d. "Services" means the activities provided by the Firm as herein provided, particulars of which are described on the reverse side hereof.
   e. "Term" means the period commencing on the Effective Date and ending on the Ending Date as set forth on the reverse side hereof.
   f. "University" means The Governors of the University of Alberta.

2. a. The University hereby retains the Firm and the Firm hereby accepts the retainer of it by the University for the purpose of providing to the University the Services.
   b. The Firm will provide the Services during the Term in accordance with, and subject to, the terms and conditions hereof and in accordance with the requirements contained in the Prime Contract.
   c. The Firm shall cause the Designated Contact to devote the necessary time and efforts to ensure the performance of the Services by the Firm.
   d. The University may terminate the retainer constituted hereby forthwith:
      (i) upon any material breach or nonperformance of the terms and conditions hereof;
      (ii) upon the cessation of employment of the Firm of the then identified Designated Contact and no new Designated Contact being approved by the University within three days thereof;
      (iii) upon the termination of the Prime Contract.

3. As payment for the Services, the University will pay to the Firm the Fee as set out on the reverse side hereof, in the manner and at the time or times set out herein and therein.

4. Nothing in this Agreement constitutes the Firm or any personnel of the Firm an employee, agent, or servant of the University, and for greater certainty the relationship of the Firm to the University is that of independent contractor. The

Exhibit 1. (*continued*)

University shall not be liable for the acts, omissions, neglect, or default of the Firm or its personnel in connection with this Agreement or the performance or nonperformance of Services.

5. The Firm will not disclose, nor shall it permit any person employed by it to disclose (except in the proper performance of the Services), any information of a private or confidential nature gained by it in the performance of the Services.

6. The Firm will not use, nor shall it permit any person employed by it to use, identifying marks of the University other than in the proper performance of the Services and in accordance with the University policy applicable thereto.

7. The Firm will render an invoice for the Fee to the University forthwith after completion of the Services or periodically as may be agreed upon, and the University will pay to the Firm the Fee of such portion thereof as is properly due.

8. Except as may otherwise be expressly agreed in writing, no amount in addition to the Fee will be payable by the University to the Firm on account of expenses or disbursements incurred by the Firm.

9. Where the Services are the teaching of a course at the University, in the case of insufficient enrollment, the University reserves the right to cancel this retainer on or before the date specified for the commencement of such course on the reverse side hereof.

10. This agreement represents the entire understanding between the parties.

11. The rights and obligations of the parties hereunder shall not be assigned or assignable.

12. This Agreement shall be interpreted under and governed by the laws of the Province of Alberta.

13. The Firm represents and warrants that the Services contracted for are directly related to the business of the Firm and are to be provided by it.

14. The Firm acknowledges that the foregoing declaration has no binding effect on the Department of National Revenue, but will be relied on by the University in determining its obligations under the Income Tax (Canada) Act and regulations thereunder.

7.   (*continued*)

    b.   Adequate compensation in the event of extra work for the consultant due to a change in the scope of the assignment or a delay caused by the client.

    c.   Limitation of consultant liability in circumstances beyond the consultant's control or due to circumstances caused by the contractor.

    d.   Nonexclusivity protection for the consultant. This will specify that the consultant may act as a consultant for others during the period of engagement with the contractor providing that this engagement does not conflict with duties or interests of the contractor.

8.   A series of clauses designed to protect the contractor. These will include some or all of the following:

    a.   Specification that the consultant shall be solely responsible for provision of any insurance deemed necessary in respect to consultant liability under the contract

    b.   A confidentiality clause to protect all information generated by the services of the consultant

    c.   Protection against subcontracting or reassigning any portion of the contract work without prior written consent

    d.   Property control of documents, drawings, specifications, reports, and pertinent papers prepared by the consultant in pursuance of the contract.

9.   A clause concerning force majeure. This clause protects both parties against claims for damages in the event of delays or failures of performance caused by occurrences beyond the control of parties affected. This sort of occurrence includes such things as decrees of government, acts of God, strikes and other concerted acts of workmen, inability to procure materials or labor, fires, floods, explosions, riots, wars, rebellion, sabotage, and atomic or nuclear incidents. It is worth noting, however, that lack of finances are not ever deemed to be a cause beyond a party's control.

10.   A termination clause specifying grounds and procedure for both sides.

11.   An audit access clause protecting both parties' access to pertinent files, data, correspondence, books, and accounting records relating to the services described in the contract.

12.   Designated representatives for contractor and consultant.

13.   A clause specifying that the contract ceases automatically with the bankruptcy or placing into receivership of either the consultant or the contractor.

14.   A clause specifying the manner of transmittal of any legal notice required between the parties.

15.   A clause outlining procedures to resolve disputes without recourse to litigation.

16. A clause stating that this formal written contract represents the entire understanding and agreement between the parties concerning the services to be provided.

These formal written contracts are always signed by the designated representative for each party and witnessed by a third party mutually agreeable to the signatories. Dates should be provided by each signatory at the time of signing.

Once the contract has been struck, the parties should maintain regular communication throughout the project in order to ensure that time lines are met, work plans are proving feasible, and cost projections are roughly in line. At the conclusion of the project, the final report that will both act as a historical account of how the project was conducted and provide the deliverables specified in the proposal must be produced. Lastly, the parties should maintain good working relations during and after the project so that follow-up work or work on further contracts can be facilitated.

References

Fisher, R., and Ury, W. *Getting to Yes: Negotiating Agreement Without Giving In.* New York: Penguin, 1983.

Keiser, T. C. "Negotiating with a Customer You Can't Afford to Lose." *Harvard Business Review,* Nov.-Dec. 1988, pp. 30–34.

Keiser, T. C. "Negotiating to Win." *Harvard Business Review,* March–April 1989, pp. 202–203.

Paton, S. M. "Negotiating Strategy and Tactics." *Corporate Accounting,* 1988, 6 (Winter), 53–58.

Shenson, H. L. *The Contract and Fee-Setting Guide for Consultants and Professionals.* New York: Wiley, 1990.

Lynn Curry is a principal in Curry Adams & Associates of Ottawa, Canada. Curry established this consulting practice in 1986, after twelve years as an academic concluding with a Rosenstadt Professorship at the University of Toronto.

The administration should use some simple procedures to manage the consultation actively and, thereby, improve the likelihood of success.

Managing the Consultation

Willard F. Enteman

This chapter suggests ways in which the administration may actively manage the consultation and gain the benefits of the consultants' expertise. The consultation itself usually introduces an additional level of complexity into what is already a complicated environment. Consultants are guests on a campus, and they should be cautious about their level of intrusiveness. Consequently, they have to follow the lead of people who know the university well, but they cannot do their job in a communication vacuum. The administration should expend extra efforts to provide the most complete and accurate communication possible for the consultants and relevant people on the campus. Good consultants want the administration to manage the consultation actively, and they will be helpful in that regard. An important early decision is the assignment of a lead consultant. She or he should be a person with maturity, experience, and unquestioned integrity. Once selected, the greater the continual involvement of the lead consultant in the entire process, the greater the chance of success. Similarly, the president should either appoint a trusted administrator as the primary representative of the university or should assume that role herself.

The lead consultant and the administration representative will find it helpful to discuss a number of topics in advance. They need to resolve their own working relationship, and they need to be clear about how they are going to communicate to the people they represent. The consultants need enough information, but not too much. They need to know what parties on the campus are to be an active part of the consultation so that they are sure to meet all relevant people. The administration needs to identify as precisely as possible the issues on which it wishes advice, and it should make clear its expectations about the kind of advice it wants. All parties should have a clear understanding of the level of confidentiality for the consultants during the consultation and in regard to the preparation and presentation of reports. With the exception of the need for open communication, most of the procedures for a consultation require balanced judgments arrived at jointly. This chapter, then, suggests methods for accomplishing all that and for ensuring the success of the consultation.

Need for Consultation Management

Some administrators treat consultations as if they might eliminate the pressures and difficulties of an administrator's life. Too many administrators apparently believe that once they have finished the difficult tasks of deciding they need consulting, finding the right consultants, and negotiating the contract, they have completed their active involvement until the consultants have finished their work and submitted a report. As a result, these administrators effectively turn the consultants loose to wander around the campus, gather whatever information might prove useful, and somehow propose solutions to problems that have resisted solution. I have participated in consultations that were important to the institution and yet in which there was almost no active role taken by the president or other senior administrator. Of course, as consultants, we did the best we could under the circumstances, but we knew that we would probably have done better if the administration had taken a more active role.

The humanities and social science faculty members, who dominate campus politics, often take a disparaging view of management in general, although they save their most irreverent comments for management consultants (and lawyers). Administrators who seek to curry favor with faculty often accept the assumptions of the rhetorical banter. As a consequence, they do not actively manage anything, including consultants who would welcome guidance. This chapter suggests that managing is an honorable endeavor and that administrators should not apologize for actively managing the consultation. I am more concerned about the failure of administrators to manage the consultation than I am about the possibility that administrators will be able to manipulate mature and experienced consultants. This chapter suggests effective methods for the administration to use in managing the consultation.

Some Preliminaries

Accountability and Authority. The president should assign focused administrative responsibility for the consultation, and, whether that assignment is to herself or a trusted administrator, she should communicate it unequivocally to the campus and the consultants. The president should be very cautious about the delegation of the final selection and supervision of consultants. All delegation depends on a degree of trust. Delegation of a consultation visit depends on the highest degree of trust because of its potential for impact beyond the campus. In one situation, an ambitious junior administrator used a consultation to undermine the credibility of the president. By the time people realized what was happening, it was too late. If the consultation is not the direct responsibility of the president, the responsible administrator should keep her well informed. For the purposes of this chapter, I shall assume the president is the responsible administrator.

Consultations start on a basis of goodwill. The administration looks forward to help with issues that concern them, and the consultants want to help. Good consultants expect the administration to manage the consultation. Obviously, they do not want anyone to manipulate them, and experienced consultants know how to deal with any such efforts whether they come from the administration or some other constituency. However, well-managed consultations will maintain their positive origins.

If the administration has selected the consultants with the care suggested in Chapter Four, the consultants will bring considerable insight and experience to the campus. However, they will not know as much about the campus as people there know, and they must adapt their expertise to the campus. The administration's challenge will be to get the best from the consultants while still actively managing the process. The consultants themselves have analogous responsibilities. If both the administration and the consultants are aware of their joint responsibilities, the consultation has a solid chance of being a success.

Administrators should disregard campus rhetoric about consultants' being administration's toadies. However, no matter how much an administration may try to distance itself from the consultants, the consultants are administrative advisers. The various constituencies will inevitably hold the administration accountable, so it should feel emboldened to use its management skills. It is difficult to refer to accountability without making a point about university administration in general. Management texts consistently argue that good management directly links authority and accountability. However, in higher education, the numerous constituencies have almost entirely delinked authority and accountability. Faculty, boards, and systems offices have extensive authority (de facto and de jure) with little accountability; presidents have intensive de jure accountability with little de facto authority. (I suggest for further study the hypothesis that the recent increase in the use of consultants correlates with the loss of authority on the part of administrators.) My plea in this chapter is that administrators not give away one more element of linked accountability and authority so that consulting will become like so much else on our campuses: expenses without benefits for achieving institutional goals.

Clearly, it makes no sense to hire consultants if the administration is going to constrain them so they cannot give their most useful advice.

However, it also makes no sense to have consultants if the situation after they leave is worse rather than better. The chances for success are much greater if the administration manages the consultation actively.

Spectra for Some Early Choices. Previous chapters have analyzed some of the choices outlined here. However, these choices are so integral to a successful relationship that it is helpful to address them briefly again. The review of the decisions also helps set the context for the assumptions of this chapter. It is good to remember that there are no hard-and-fast rules that we can apply. However, we have to decide, and we should do it explicitly rather than letting events take over. The careful consideration of these issues shows the consultants that the administration means to be an active participant in the management of the consultation.

Complex or Focused. Consultations can range from the very complex to the very focused. They may be as simple as helping the institution decide whether to purchase or lease the next mainframe computer. They may be as complex as helping the institution decide what its mission should be. This chapter assumes that the consultation we are considering is complex and involves recommendations for developing and implementing institutional goals. The most important difference is that in a sharply focused consultation, the administration needs to keep the consultants on task. Otherwise, they may wander into unassigned territories and cause trouble. The administration may invite the consultants to suggest privately further investigation and even further consultations. However, the consultants should stay with the task at hand. Consultations about complex issues need to have mutually recognized boundaries, but they will naturally reach into unanticipated areas. The administration should tell the consultants to discuss moving beyond agreed-on boundaries before acting.

Analytical or Action Oriented. In some cases, the university wants an analytically oriented consultation. The consultants analyze a situation and prepare a report. They do not participate in the implementation of the recommendations. In other consultations, the university expects the consultants to be change agents, often breaking political impasses. Most complex consultations will involve elements of each, but there is likely to be an emphasis. The president and the consultants should understand and accept the emphasis and be in close touch with each other if they believe they should change it. Consultations are usually more analytical than action oriented. There are substantial dangers with the latter, since the consultants cannot know the campus well. Nevertheless, some consultations of that nature have been notably successful. This chapter emphasizes analytically oriented consultations. Administrators should adjust for other cases. I suggest two special cautions for administrators considering more action-oriented consultations. They need to manage such consultations even more carefully, and they need to reassure themselves of the maturity of the consultants.

One Time or Long Term. There has been an increasing use of longer-term consultations with repeated visits and a continuing relationship. That is generally a positive development. It helps consultants gain a longer-term view and deters them from thinking that they have to solve all the problems at one time. Longer-term consultations give the administration and the consultants time to correct for any deficiencies and to deal with misunderstandings. However, since long-term consultations are still unusual, this chapter assumes that consultants will spend only a few days on campus.

Team or Individual. Some consultations involve only a single person. Others involve a group of people, often called a team. Sharply focused consultations may not warrant the expense and complication of a team. However, since campuses are so complex, the team approach is generally preferable because it can take advantage of a number of perspectives. This chapter assumes that the consultation under consideration will involve a team that includes a lead consultant as one of the members.

The appointment of the lead consultant is very important. Team members will not have worked together before. An important task of the lead consultant will be to coordinate the team. Members must work together effectively and stay focused on the task at hand. It is very important that there be clear communication and mutual respect between the president and the lead consultant. A visit to the campus by the lead consultant before the entire team's visit is advisable. Where possible, it is also advisable to have the lead consultant involved in selecting the rest of the team. However, in the end this is the president's project. A good lead consultant will know when she has pressed her case as far as she should take it.

If the lead consultant does not know all the members of the team, the administration should give her the resources to meet those she does not know before coming to the campus. In this context, it is not advisable to use consulting novices as lead consultants. Consultants should serve first as members of teams before assuming the responsibilities of leadership. The leadership task is qualitatively more demanding than that of being a team member. Having an experienced person as the lead consultant will go a long way toward ensuring a successful consultation.

The Management of Consultations

Communication

Communication is important in all management. It is critical in successful consultation because of the time compression. Paraphrasing a favorite slogan of realtors, we might say that the three most important rules of constructive consultant working relationships are communication, communication, and communication. If the administration does not have the time and energy to communicate actively with the consultants, it should eliminate or reschedule the consultation. The administration must make sure that the channels of communication are constantly open. That is especially important while the consultants are on campus. The lead consultant and the president should know how to contact each other quickly if anything begins to go wrong. The president should know the lead consultant's schedule, and the lead consultant should stick with the schedule or tell the president's office otherwise. When the team is on campus, the president should plan to meet each day with the lead consultant.

The administration should be sure the consultants have an adequate amount of material to review before they arrive on campus. The consultants must have the material early enough to read it carefully. The administration should not flood the consultants with too much information. Communication is a process of selective balance. An indiscriminate flood of material is not helpful for the consultants. At the beginning of the visit, everyone should have a detailed discussion of the information that the university has provided. The administration will gain an impression of how well the team members have prepared, and the team will have an opportunity to ask for further clarification and information.

Campus Constituency Involvement

The administration should also communicate with those parts of the campus that the consultation is most likely to affect. Where possible, it is advisable to involve the appropriate people on the campus in the decision to bring in consultants. People on the campus will not adopt solutions to problems they do not believe exist. Even the most prestigious consultants will not be able to overcome that fact. Potentially valuable consultations have foundered because the people responsible for implementation did not believe the recommendations solved any problem they could identify. People usually hire consultants because they believe there is a problem. The more people share that belief, the greater the chance that those responsible for implementation will actually carry out the suggestions. So far as possible and reasonable, it is helpful to have people also participate in selecting the consultants. In the end, the consultation belongs to the president, and he should feel the confidence of knowing how to select people for the consultation. However, if there is an opportunity for congruence and a sense of involvement, that will increase the chances of a genuinely constructive relationship.

Need Identification

Chapter Two has already identified the importance of having the institution identify the issue it wants addressed. It has also given some helpful guidelines for identifying the needs. It is referred to again here because it is part of the important communication link between the campus and the consultants.

No one can be more definitive about the need than the facts will allow. Sometimes there is little more to go on than a sense that people feel something is not right. They want some experienced outsiders to examine the situation and either reassure them or suggest some other course of action. Sometimes the people on the campus can only identify symptoms and cannot discover the underlying causes. None of that is a reason for concern. Successful consultations have proceeded with just that small amount of information. In other cases, in contrast, everyone is clear about what the problem and the need are. (Of course, they may be wrong, and one task of good consultants will be to tell them when they are wrong and how they should change their perceptions.) The communication between the university and the consultants needs to be as clear as the facts will allow. It is as bad for the administration to feign clarity about need as it is for it to pretend it does not have any well-formed opinions. Good consultants can be very helpful. However, the administration should not think consultants can produce miracles or that they are mind readers. Consultants are not a substitute for administrative work.

Common Problems and How to Avoid Them

There are a number of opportunities for difficulty that the administration should recognize. In general, the best way to avoid them is to discuss them explicitly with the lead consultant and be sure there is a common understanding. Conversations of this nature will not insult good consultants, and if the conversations appear to insult others, the administration has good cause for concern.

No Surprises. Perhaps the most important unwritten rule of many consultations and yet the one that may supersede all others is that the consultants should provide no surprises. I do not mean to preclude the likelihood that consultants may make some unexpected discoveries, and I do not mean that consultants should not report those discoveries. I mean, rather, that they should communicate such discoveries privately, and the public report on them should never come as a surprise to the administration. In a sense, that duty falls most heavily on the shoulders of the lead consultant, but the administration should let the consultants know it expects them to fulfill that responsibility. The role of university administrator is difficult enough without having people the president retains become part of her problems rather than part of her solutions.

Confidentiality. Higher education is a small and largely closed community. It is easy for an experienced person to extrapolate from limited information and identify an institution. Administrators should be sure the consultants they hire will keep whatever level of confidentiality the administration wishes and should discuss the topic of confidentiality with the consultants early in their contact. In general, I recommend that after delivery of the final report to the university, consultants destroy all their records. That way, if someone tries to involve one of the consultants in a dispute later, she can truthfully say that she does not have a copy of the materials.

Exit Interviews: Private. The president should arrange a private final exit interview with at least the lead consultant. If there is to be a more public exit interview, the president should know what the consultants will say. The private interview is a last opportunity for the president to express privately his own opinions about what the team may decide to say. The lead consultant can also make last-minute changes. In addition, the team can give helpful advice that may be beyond the scope of the consultation. In this context, I need to note those states that operate under "sunshine" legislation. The administration needs to tell the consultants about any restrictions on the reporting process.

Exit Interviews: Public. Presumably, there will be a public exit interview open to many people. In general, the preferred procedure is for the administration to invite all interested people. By the time of such an interview, the lead consultant should have enough acquaintance with the university that she will not step on any toes unnecessarily. By virtue of the private exit interview, the president will prepare an appropriate response. A complex consultation involves a broad portion of the campus. They should know how the visit has concluded, even though the lead consultant should say that the findings are tentative and subject to revision.

Written Reports. Getting the written report can be a frustrating aspect of consultations. The longer the actual report takes to arrive, the more time campus storytellers have to gossip about what they heard in the exit interview. If that lapse is too long, the final report will be useless no matter how much it may diverge from the on-campus rumors. Here I suggest four devices for speeding up the arrival of the final written report. I purposefully leave aside the obvious device of not paying the consultants until they submit the final report. I would recommend that as a matter of course, and the administration should make that provision in the contract, as Chapter Five indicates. My concern here is to move beyond contractual relationships in an effort to manage the consultation effectively.

Getting Results on Time. Many consultants have responsible lives on their own campuses, and once they return, those responsibilities take their attention no matter how much they wish otherwise. It is often useful to invite the lead consultant to spend an extra day wherever she is staying during the campus visit. In that way, she can work undisturbed putting together the first draft of the report. Obviously, to make the process work effectively, it makes sense for the university to be sure the lead consultant has the technical and personnel support necessary to get the job done. The lead consultant should complete the first draft while the experiences are still fresh in her mind, and she should give the president a copy of the draft before she leaves.

Review of Early Drafts. The administration should arrange with the lead consultant to have early drafts of the report sent directly to the president for review. Documentation from a consultation takes on a finality that is very difficult to dispel later. For academics, words are important. Phrases that are innocent on one campus can be explosive on another. Presidents should make detailed comments on early drafts of the report to the lead consultant. Lead consultants should be confident enough to accept the president's requested changes when they are convincing and to reject them when they are not convincing.

Role of Lead Consultant. This section is late in the chapter because of its logical connection to the lead consultant's reporting responsibilities. However, the administration should deal with this topic from the beginning of the consultation. The president should make it clear that in the end she wants a report that the lead consultant endorses. The job of the lead consultant is to wring as much consensus as possible out of the team. Talented lead consultants can often find consensus where others cannot. However, the consulting activity is very intensive, and sometimes the team cannot develop a consensus. Reports that include minority report sections usually do not serve the university well. If the lead consultant has final responsibility for the report, she can give due acknowledgment to those areas in which there was not consensus. She can also produce a coherent report that will arrive on time. If the lead consultant has to check each word with each member of the team, the university may have to wait a long time for the report. There have even been situations of no report at all.

Final Written Report. Once the president has a first draft, and the lead consultant has clear responsibility for the production of the final report, completed copy is likely to come along in a timely fashion. If it does not, at least the president will have a copy she can use in the meantime (which may explain why the final one comes along quickly). Inexperienced consultants, especially, think that they will write a better report after they have had time for more reflection. However, it is equally true that the separation of time makes it more difficult to write the report.

Conclusion

This chapter has focused on the responsibilities of administration for ensuring a successful consultation. The consultants themselves—and especially the lead consultant—have analogous responsibilities. I have spent much of my professional career both as a consultant and as a senior administrator retaining consultants. I have derived the suggestions in this chapter from discussions with many other people and from experience on both sides of the desk.

I believe the nature of university administration is undergoing profound change in colleges and universities, but we do not know the outcome. The days of the autocratic president who involved himself in everything from disciplining undergraduates to hiring faculty are gone. The externally motivated drive of the late 1960s and the 1970s to make universities more "businesslike" fortunately failed to take hold. (Its only element of continuing success may be in the area of tuition: like fashionable businesses, prestigious colleges and universities tested the market to see what increased price levels it would bear. It is ironic that some of the voices calling for universities to become more businesslike objected when universities did precisely that.) Except in unimportant ways, universities do not resemble businesses.

More recently, internal and external forces have made universities resemble political instrumentalities. Without acknowledging that shift explicitly, we have nevertheless done so implicitly by referring regularly to constituencies. Presidents have to negotiate with boards, alumni associations, systems offices, legislators, governors, unions, faculty senates, student organizations, and staff associations. The collective wisdom of all these constituencies is inconsistent, and, typically, their interest in the university is only to use it as a means to advance their other agenda. Perhaps the only point of agreement of the competing constituents is that they want "leadership" from the president. However, they do not want to exercise their responsibilities for what James MacGregor Burns (1978) calls "followership" in his definitive book, Leadership. It is no wonder that our campuses, like our political instrumentalities, have moved to a kind of stalemate in which each constituency negates the other, and together they accomplish little of significance. A dominant issue on campuses currently, and one that involves many consultations, is "governance." The word itself has become a euphemism for temporizing. However, universities, unlike political instrumentalities, do not exist only to give competing interests a forum for debate and resolution. They exist to accomplish something: the promotion of learning.

Presidents try desperately to ride this multiheaded animal, which veers in many different directions at once. Of course, there still are some autocratic presidents, and our concern about them is suitable (though in this book we need not pay much attention to them, because they are unlikely to risk retaining consultants). We should have even greater concern for the plethora of presidents and administrators whose constituencies tie their hands so much that they do little of importance or are too timid to try. Ultimately, higher education has to sort out its decision-making processes on some new and more satisfactory basis. In the meantime, presidents and others have found that consultations can bring a useful perspective that can give some reasonable—and reasoned—guidance without political entanglements and private agenda. I suspect that no matter how higher education restructures its decision-making processes, there will be a significant place for consultations. This chapter should help administrators and consultants establish a productive relationship that will promote learning.

Reference

Burns, J. M. *Leadership*. New York: Harper & Row, 1978.

Willard F. Enteman has been a consultant for numerous colleges and universities. He has served as provost and faculty member at Union College, New York, and at Rhode Island College and as president of Bowdoin College, Maine. He recently returned to his faculty position as professor of philosophy at Rhode Island College and continues consulting regularly.

Good consultant feedback is evidence-based insight. The
administrator needs to prepare for hearing and acting on it.

Handling Consultant Feedback

Jack Lindquist

We all love and need applause. If it cannot be a Broadway curtain call, a pat on the shoulder or a "Nice going" will do just fine.

Remember the last time you got (or gave) either on campus?

We all need criticism, too: the constructive kind, that is, not cheap or behind-the-back shots. Those do nobody any good, including the shooter. What we need is professionally constructive criticism, the kind that points us toward feasible improvement without withering us personally.

If your college is like the ones in which I have worked or consulted the last twenty years, constructive criticism is as rare as applause. Nevitt Sanford's (1967) wise advice regarding teaching—to join nurturance and challenge in a mix appropriate to the person of each learner—seems to me even less practiced in administration.

Applause and criticism are, of course, feedback. For professional feedback, enter your consultant.

She or he may be on staff in an office such as our editor's. Sometimes better for appearance of social distance and therefore neutrality is the consultant who arrives by plane from at least a hundred miles away. I recall consulting a division of my own university only when I was returning from elsewhere so the team could pick me up at the airport like a proper consultant.

In selecting the consultant whose feedback you hope to use, expertise in whatever you want looked into is necessary. As important, however, is your sense that here you have a candid but kind friend, someone who will tell you the things that are hard for you to hear, for you need to hear them, but who will say them supportively, with at least a sprinkling of the applause you surely deserve.

Forms of Feedback

There are really just two general forms of consultant feedback: the formal report (usually written) and the in-process observation, given while watching you, and perhaps your colleagues, in action. Both are important sources of insight, so I usually include both in my own consultations.

The formal report may have any number of topics: market analyses, success-after-graduation studies, analyses of management style and effectiveness, studies of plant use and obsolescence or of the institution's financial health. These reports may take six months and be costly (good consultants are not cheaper than good deans), or they may be the result of, say, a two-day examination of existing evidence.

Either way, consultant reports are not like academic papers that you present at conferences. The fundamental difference is that consultant reports are *about their audience* and aim to *encourage change in their audience's behavior*. A consultant's effectiveness rests not on how well received her reports are (although material success may come of that); the test is how useful and used to improve things the feedback is.

In-process observation is often nerve wracking for the client. Who dares have a professional observer right there watching you teach or chair a meeting? Unfortunately, it is very difficult for a consultant to provide useful feedback about a behavior she cannot directly observe. The equivalent might be a riding trainer who suggests ways to improve your fence jumping without watching you try it.

My advice, therefore, is to invite the in-process observation and feedback, but with provisos I mention later.

About Formal Reports

Some consultant feedback requires the depth and breadth of a written report. A market analysis must depict the available markets, your institution's current niche, available evidence regarding the shift or expansion of that niche, and how to go about it. A success-after-graduation study contains evidence regarding the residual learning and effectiveness "out there" of an acceptable sample of your graduates. A management analysis usually benefits from systematic interviews of managers and the managed.

Systematic evidence and analysis are what you are asking of your consultant. But first:

Request an *executive summary*. I call it the Ike principle, because I first heard of the idea when President Eisenhower used it. Academicians, like politicians, are very busy and are inundated with boring papers; however, they will read a brief summary of the evidence.

Request a *data backup* to the summary, neatly presenting all the evidence anyone needs to understand and weigh the summary. Here I urge exposition, not analysis, for a simple but vital reason: you want to weigh the consultant's evidence to draw your analysis, not the consultant's, for what you conclude is the key to any changes you make.

You may request a separate *consultant analysis*. Consultants have opinions on everything, and sometimes they are helpful. However, take pains to avoid arguing over the consultant's analyses. Argue over the evidence.

Feedback to Groups

If the report is a major one and is aimed at colleagues as well, say, the admissions staff on marketing and the faculty on learning outcomes, engage this broader audience with you in the feedback.

One easy and effective means is the *feedback workshop*. Ask your consultant to design with you a two-day event for you and your colleagues. Also ask a small group of well-respected colleagues to join you and your consultant as the workshop planning team. If research is part of the feedback, be sure to get a faculty member who does that kind of research on the team so that others might accept its worth.

Invite to the workshop everyone concerned with the topic, but also get "opinion leaders" and "authorities" (Lindquist, 1978), those who can make things happen afterward. Here is where the agricultural extension agent's networking tricks, such as face-to-face invitation and "I'll pick you up on the way," are a lot more effective than engraved invitations.

A week before the event, send out the report—no earlier, or it will get buried; no later, or "I didn't get it" becomes the sad refrain. A brief cover letter from the planning team raising questions the report might answer can help generate interest. Also, be sure to bring extra copies to the first session.

I like feedback events over two days because conscientious participants tend to realize after the first day that although we are talking about the issues, we are not agreeing on what should be done and who is going to do it. A second day on just these matters benefits from a night to sleep (or not) on it. If two full days are hard to come by, try an afternoon session followed by a dinner, then a morning session the next day.

I also advocate small-group work. Large groups (much over a dozen) can listen, but they cannot equally participate and cannot build the rapport it takes to find agreement or, even tougher, to volunteer some follow-up effort. If the first day has a general introduction, then small-group discussion facilitated by team members, with the challenge of identifying four or five things needing improvement, it will be a productive day. I urge volunteer recorders to outline the group's points on newsprint, then report them orally in the next day's general session.

One ingredient I believe should never be absent from workshops is social time together for participants. A reception, a dinner, coffee breaks, silly or serious award ceremonies, certainly refreshments in the back of the room: all these build the friendly social fabric necessary for working well together.

Action Planning and Reaction

Action plans mean action after the workshop, and that should mean scheduling a follow-up session (or two, or one a month). Just as students get serious before exams, so do professionals get busy before a public meeting in which they are to report on all the things they previously said they would do. I strongly advise that the first follow-up session be announced before people leave the feedback workshop. I also advise inviting your consultant to the follow-up. One of the most accurate reflections on consulting I ever heard was that the key to effective consulting is showing up. Ask your consultant to show up for the feedback session, and a useful session should ensue.

Handling Interpersonal Feedback

Next is the scary part: feedback directly to you or others by a consultant who has been observing your teaching, committee chairing, solicitation of funds, reception of student protesters, or any other of the constant variety of interpersonal work administrators face every day.

Clients can feel helpless in the face of human relations consultants. They fear having every real and imagined flaw exposed to all their colleagues, and who needs that?

Nobody. No first-rate consultant would ever do something so destructive, even if she could. To be sure, contract your consultant's interpersonal feedback so that you can feel more sure that you can survive and even benefit from it.

One thing to contract is the focus of the observation and feedback. For example, you may have heard from others that you do not listen. That is a familiar complaint, especially about people in authority. "Could you watch how well I listen to this group?" is something a consultant knows how to manage. Were it asked of me, I would watch for attending behavior on your part. (Do you look at whoever is speaking with an expression of interest I can describe?) I would listen for your reiteration of and building on others' comments. I would listen for your "Can you say more about that?" or "I don't understand (or agree with this part). Could you explain that again?" And I would surely watch for attending behavior by you after that second question, which so easily can be a set-up if you think there is a hole in some colleague's argument.

A second topic for negotiation is how your consultant feeds back. Professionals tend to feed back the easy material first, mostly applause or small but useful technical hints, say, on how to keep a discussion in focus.

Leadership, which is the issue here, tends to be more difficult and personal than the technical side. My introvert's shyness, and therefore not very social kind of leadership, gets interpreted as aloofness. I know that now, after many human relations workshops, but I would have shrunk into the floor if some consultant had told me about it in front of my staff in 1970.

Consultants usually are quite willing to agree with you to start light and get into the heavy feedback when you feel ready for it. At first, that may mean watching your interaction, then "debriefing" you in private.

However, if you want your consultant's interpersonal feedback shared with your administrative team, committee, or class, you will need to agree to a stage in which the consultant's feedback to you is in their presence. This is the old platoon leader adage, "I wouldn't ask you to experience anything I wouldn't"; interpersonal feedback is easier when the boss is there taking his or her lumps with us. I still recall as my best day as a college president the one in which my friend, the wonderful human relations consultant Charlie Seashore, hauled me out in the middle of Goddard's faculty and administration to point out, by "becoming" me, how cynical I sounded. (I was not, of course, but I immediately felt a negative affect I had no wish to stir.)

Remember to ask no more emotional risk of your students, faculty, or staff than you do of yourself. If you want feedback in private, leave the room when the consultant shares observations on the group's behavior with them. Do not cheat by trying later to get the consultant to tell you what she said to them. Such tactics are no fair and no good even in the short run.

Once you and your consultant have worked out how she or he is to give interpersonal feedback, it becomes time to receive it.

There are two factors that you should practice and that are vital to planned change. One is *openness*. The other is *ownership*.

Openness takes work. It means opening yourself, or yourselves, to fact and opinion new or foreign or even disturbing to you. Your consultants probably will advise you to suspend disbelief, to open your eyes and ears. During the feedback, ask questions only to clarify, understand, and appreciate what you are hearing. Argument, if necessary, comes later. The job first is to give this feedback all the attention and interest you can.

Often, the above comes hard. Another consultant, or a skilled and sensitive member of your group, may need to referee at first, reminding you and others to understand and appreciate now, evaluate later. This is a good idea even if you have a consultant who mostly hears and sees what is not there on issues about which only she seems to care.

Ownership means that the feedback and the related problem solving are yours, not the consultant's. "This is my [our] insight into issues of import to me [us] pursuant to this institution's goals, and I am [we are] deciding what to do about it."

To obtain ownership of consultant feedback, you need a consultant who believes that her or his job is to facilitate your inquiry and action, not to instruct it. Ask about this. It will probably mean gathering data with or coached by the consultant, analyzing it with the consultant's help, and making and carrying out action plans the same way.

You may want more directive consultation, which is actually easier to find than the facilitative sort. However, I do not believe it works well for long.

Digesting and weighing feedback take more time. A coffee break may suffice for simple feedback. Intensive feedback will take longer. A long walk, a night to stew, perhaps even a couple of weeks to weigh it all may be the fastest route, depending on what was said.

The important point for *use* of feedback is that a time is scheduled (with the consultant, at least) to declare what you, the client, will or will not do to follow up the feedback.

"Nothing. It's horse pucky," is surely okay to a Saratoga horseperson. But "I do want to listen better to my staff" or "we do need to figure out why succeeding here academically is not much of a predictor of future success" or "I now know staff members are unhappy with the way this place treats them, and I'm going to do something about it" are conclusions deserving follow-up. The next step, therefore, is an action plan no different from the one described earlier. If you are the feedback recipient, make the plan with your consultant, including the date you and she or he set for a follow-up session.

You may not anticipate one helpful use of your consultant. What if your behavior change receives a negative response or becomes so personally straining that you do not quite do it? Such is likely in the midst of change. A consultant, familiar with such but not as embroiled in it, can be an invaluable guide and listening post during the change itself.

Summary

Consultant feedback is—at least it should be—professional, evidence-based insight into the good and bad and indifferent of your work. It can be expected in one or both of two forms: a formal report of the consultant's findings or oral feedback following direct observation. The range of such feedback includes the whole of your work, from a close look at your interpersonal style to a sweeping assessment of your institution's demographics.

Handling consultant feedback well (meaning you get useful feedback and use it) is not easy, if for no other reason than that it is about you, so natural defenses rise. A consultant sensitive to the emotional side of handling feedback and facilitative of your doing the handling can go a long way toward the balance of nurturance and challenge that marks good feedback, like good teaching and administrating.

References

Lindquist, J. *Strategies for Change*. Washington, D.C.: Council of Independent Colleges, 1978.

Sanford, N. *Why Colleges Fail: The Study of the Student as a Person*. San Francisco: Jossey-Bass, 1967.

Jack Lindquist is immediate past president of Goddard College, in Plainfield, Vermont, author or coauthor of five volumes on collegiate planned change, and consultant to dozens of colleges.

*Substantive institutional change can only be accomplished by faculty
and staff who, themselves, have changed.*

Managing Change Creatively

Robert J. Toft

The consultant has given his or her recommendations and departed. In the
words of Basil Fawlty, "[That was a] piece of cake! Now comes the tricky
bit" (Cleese and Booth, 1988, p. 303). The goodwill, warm feelings, and
spirit of cooperation that usually mark the involvement with the consultant
are now a memory. When you look around and find that your colleagues
are the same, the students have not changed, and the politics of the place
still operate as before, you may wonder how you are going to manage the
change that has been started. The purpose of this chapter is to give you
some tips and a nudge to get you going.

Colleges Are Conservative

In his recent book on college administration, Birnbaum (1988) explained
that colleges are very conservative institutions and are resistant to change.
The sharing of authority between the faculty and board of trustees means
that there is considerable overlap in perceived power and that each com-
ponent acts cautiously with respect to the other. Concerns about community beliefs and feelings toward the institution ("town-gown relationships"),
inflexibility of financial resources (and of donors of those resources), inter-
institutional comparisons of prestige, and the impossibility of defining the
"product" of the enterprise in the words of institutional tenets all constitute
constraints on the institution that move it toward a conservative stance.

Birnbaum (1988) believes that organizational cultures that set norms
for various behaviors and processes exist in the institution. These cultures
have their own symbols and myths and help to establish a consensus on
appropriate behavior. Unlike explicit mechanisms such as rules, regulations,

job descriptions, and chains of command, cultures are "implicit, unobtrusive, and for the most part not subject to purposeful manipulation by administrators," says Birnbaum (1988, p. 80).

Change Is Difficult

Because of these conservative elements, there is great difficulty for the faculty group or administrator who wishes to make a significant change in any part of the academic program, and there is relatively little hope that it will survive if implemented. In preparation for this writing, I called a friend who has been a dean, academic vice-president, and president at several different institutions. I asked about the fate of any number of specific innovative programs started at the various campuses. "They have all collapsed," was the response. I have asked this question of others and have reviewed a number of change efforts in which I have been involved. The answer, in most cases, is the same.

I was on the campus of a liberal arts college, evaluating the final year of a $1-plus million grant designed to impact the entire curriculum, when the word came that the college had just received another $1-plus million award from another funding source to do a different type of all-campus project. The faculty, who were totally fatigued by the requirements of the first grant, were actually stunned by news of the second. I am confident that the changes wrought by both awards were quickly lost.

To paraphrase Machiavelli, the innovator has for supporters those who are disaffected by the current situation but are only lukewarm to the new idea. The detractors are all those who have done well under the current system and do not wish to see any upset in the status quo.

Major Change Does Occur

Let me hasten to point out that change is possible and that you should continue reading. In the early 1970s, Alverno College in Wisconsin embarked on a radical change in its curriculum and mode of assessment. A small Catholic women's college, Alverno was faced with enrollment problems. Furthermore, Alverno's graduates were not moving into positions commensurate with their education (a phenomenon now known as the "glass ceiling"). Basically, the college redesigned the entire curriculum, modes of teaching, and methods of evaluating student performance. Today, Alverno continues to be a success story. To make such a change required skill, dedication, teamwork, and a strong motivating force (survival). Each of us can point to at least one example where significant change has taken place and where the results are both positive and permanent. However, you may be surprised to find that the skills needed for bringing about such changes are not present in most players

but must be learned. The remainder of this chapter deals with the identification and mode of acquisition of those skills.

Conditions Affecting Institutional Change

A New Type of Leadership. Birnbaum (1988), in speaking about the
role of the higher education manager, says that academic administration
may consist largely of symbolic action. He points out that, while we speak
of rational managers, our institutional administrators seem to emphasize
intuition rather than using either quantitative data or new management
techniques. Consequently, they often respond to political influences. Lack-
ing the skills or authority for true participative growth, managers tend to
rely on crisis management, thus throwing various groups and factions into
conflict with no avenue for reasoned resolution.

It is important for you as a manager of change to focus on acquiring
the skills necessary to get beyond crisis management and to become a
manager of learning for innovative change. For example, you must develop
a style for helping others to examine institutional goals and personal beliefs
as part of the legitimate process of problem solving. You will need to
improve your ability to both encourage and manage interpersonal conflict—
allowing participants to ventilate their fears and anxieties—in an atmosphere where such behaviors are a valued part of the growth process. You
will have to be alert to catch statements not based on observable data and
to assist in both the acquisition of such data and the public testing of
group inferences. Finally, you must find ways to reward such open participation until the group members have internalized the new approach and
have become advocates. By the end of this chapter, you will have some
guideposts to help you on your journey toward that goal.

Faculty Are the Key. In my opinion, the focal point for change on a
campus is the individual faculty person. Each person, if motivated, can
grow and change. If enough persons are moved in the same direction, they
can form a nucleus for bringing about significant institutional change. I will
focus more on the interaction among the players because of my strong
belief in the skills needed for working with people. My emphasis is on
understanding the motivations and points of resistance of those with whom
you must work and those who will be affected by the change you are
instituting.

Let me turn now to a discussion of some organizational and environmental factors affecting campus change. Regardless of our abilities as
change agents, we must be attuned to the campus setting in both general
and specific ways. Before discussing the individual players in the change, I
will speak of the institution as an entity, recognizing that such a personifi-
cation has definite shortcomings.

Four Institutional Models. Birnbaum (1988) divides American colleges and universities into four models, depending on the type of administration that prevails: collegial, bureaucratic, political, and anarchical.

In the collegial model, he has summarized some rules for administrators to follow: live up to the norms of the group, conform to group expectations of leadership, use established channels of communication, do not give an order that will not be obeyed, listen, reduce status differences, and encourage self-control.

The bureaucratic institution is characterized by heavy reliance on lines of authority and lines of communication, with complex organizational charts for every office and function. Location on a chart signals importance of an office. All offices have codified rules and regulations, with written job descriptions and rules for behavior and performance.

In the political model, there is competition for power and resources. Power is diffused and changeable. Control is through coalition building. Different groups in the institution develop issues of concern, leaving alone the concerns of other groups, says Birnbaum. The president uses persuasion and diplomacy as her or his principal tools for managing.

The anarchical model, Birnbaum says, is represented by a major, prestigious state university. "An organized anarchy exhibits three characteristics: problematic goals, an unclear technology, and fluid participation" (Birnbaum, 1988, p. 154). A major issue in decision making for this type of institution is the uncertain coupling of one issue with another. Because various constituencies have related or competing needs and desires, a decision made in favor of one group may call down the wrath of several other groups. Because of the diffused power, it is not easy for a single individual (president) or group to set firm policy.

To manage change in an institution, one must be aware of the ways decisions are reached, resources are distributed, and appointments are made. Even if you are unfamiliar with Birnbaum's typology, you can probably at least describe the basic operating system in which you are embedded. Your choices as manager will be tempered by your knowledge of how these critical elements are dealt with internally. Reading Birnbaum gives a refreshing simplification to this complex topic and may provide sustenance, or at least comic relief, for those of you who are feeling "stuck" and immobile.

Conditions for Successful Change. In his work on organizational development, Richard Beckhard (1969) has developed a list of ten conditions necessary for successful organizational change. In slightly modified form, they are as follows: (1) there is pressure for change (internal or external); (2) some strategic person is "hurting"; (3) someone is willing to do a real diagnosis of the problem; (4) there is leadership (consultant, staff, line executive); (5) there is collaborative problem identification between faculty and administration; (6) there is a willingness to take risks in trying new forms of relationships; (7) there is a realistic, long-term perspective; (8) participants are willing to face the data and change the situation; (9) there will be rewards for the *effort* of changing and improvement as well as for short-term results; and (10) there will be tangible intermediate results.

It is interesting to note that Beckhard considers the motivation for change to be that of the stick rather than the carrot. Pressure and someone's "hurting" are the first two considerations. The most challenging conditions, in my judgment, are the collaborative problem identification, the risk in forming new relationships, and facing the data. Your skills as the manager of change will be tested in all three of these areas.

Institutional Investment. The level of institutional investment affects both the targets for change and the degree of change that can be expected. This investment will be in the form of time spent by the change agent and the learning achieved by those affected by the change. Change involves procedures, policies, and people. Of course, the three are basically inseparable. However, we tend to isolate them in our planning. In general, if you have little time and resources and a limited scope to your project, then you can try changing procedures. You can easily enlist the aid of many in a project that appears to be principally a mechanistic venture.

The thought of changing policies tugs at bigger anxieties among those affected, necessitating more extensive planning, review, coordination, discussion, and compromise. If you tramp on my routines (procedural change), my ego gets hurt; when you stomp around in my intellectual garden (policy change), my professional image gets damaged. Since my professional image is seen by colleagues, it must be defended more vigorously and more publicly.

Divorcing either procedural or policy change from the people who will be affected will result in failure to successfully implant the change. If you can bring the people to understand the change, participate in its design and evolution, and feel a sense of ownership for it, then the needed policies and procedures will flow from the group and individuals. The planning and implementation will take longer, but the change will become embedded in the fabric of the institution rather than simply be plastered over the existing patterns.

The Manager and Change

There are many ways in which you, the manager of change, can make use of your knowledge of people and their systems to shape the conditions so there will be constructive engagement of most persons who will be affected by the change.

Your Own Motivation. Sometime, early in the process, take a hard look at your own motivations for initiating and implementing the project that you desire to carry out. Reasons might include rewards (better education, fewer problems, smoother operation, professional recognition, growth in the institution, preparation for higher position), emotional commitment to the idea, and rational commitment to the project. Be clear about your own reasons. As you become aware of your own motivations and share your thoughts with others who will be involved, you increase your own confidence in the project and send reassuring messages to your colleagues.

If you are having difficulty confronting the emotional content of your motivation, you will almost certainly fail to get commitment from others. The changes that you seek cannot take place solely as a rational-intellectual activity. Unfortunately, most of us have been "beat up" for years when we have allowed our emotions to emerge in academic planning, and we have learned to describe all plans in serious tones. We deny our emotions and so are ruled by them.

Openness as a Means. I do not wish to leave the notion that emotional exposure is an end; it is only a means. Argyris has said it nicely: "Candor and openness are not the ultimate purposes of learning. They are conditions that enable people to reflect on the reasoning behind their actions and to design and execute mini-experiments so that they can test old action strategies and create new ones. Along with reflections on their reasoning processes and experimentation, it is important for people to express their feelings because catharsis under prolonged states of failure and threat may act as a safety valve. Clearing the emotional air can increase the probability of effective reflection and experimentation" (1982, p. 169).

In a recent television interview, a welfare counselor said that it is a mistake to tell a welfare person to first become educated or trained and then to find a job. The person must first have a job—and then the self-esteem will grow, allowing training or education to follow. All college personnel suffer loss of self-esteem because of the authority structure. Most hide it. If you can help them rebuild that sense of self-worth, it will kindle a fire in them that will blaze with appreciation and commitment. That is how change comes about!

Your Learning Curve. Determine your necessary "learning curve" for the change. What new information came from the consultation? Has it been digested, assimilated, shared? What new information do you still need to assemble before implementation is complete? Who are the best sources for this information? Remember that those affected by the change need to be included in the learning process. Work to develop their collective expertise.

Timing. Think about the timing of the change. Will it be gradual or sudden? Every person affected has a notion of the proper time line for a given change. Bring out those different opinions and examine each one. They will tell you a lot about the resistance you face. Be willing to extend or shorten the implementation time.

Opposition. Who will be opposed to the changes? We have already dealt with some of the reasons why those affected will oppose you. Open opposition is easier to deal with than the many forms of covert opposition.

Passive-aggressive behavior can sap your energies and those of the team with whom you are working. Some people will go along with whatever you propose out of a desire to please you and be a good sport. Those supporters will desert you in the long run because they are not committed to the change. Often there is a general hierarchical threat—a threat to authority. I once wrote a short piece about the campus "grant wizard." To everyone's dismay, this person is very successful in attracting money, thereby giving him- or herself a kind of autonomy that threatens almost everyone. Maintaining the status quo allows everyone to adjust, so any threats or problems lie hidden. With change, all these old hurts and perceived injustices come bubbling to the surface, often surprising the change agents, since the outbursts seem poorly aimed with respect to the projects being undertaken. It is not dissimilar to commuters who snap at their spouses because of frustration with rush-hour drivers.

Get help in analyzing the opposition to the project. Ask others on your team to express any opposition or questions they have. Getting them to ventilate their feelings will give you valuable information needed to plan your approach for acceptance of the change. If you get opposition, do not ignore it. Deal with it openly—it will not go away of its own accord.

Stewardship. What you are attempting will require new work groups or new responsibilities for those that already exist. New group norms must be established. Do not hesitate to ask others how they think the process should go. This will not be seen as weakness, especially if you are sincere in asking.

The implementation of a change has an energy of its own. The participants are involved and usually excited about the improvement. Once the change is in place, especially when new people are brought into the already changed institution, there is a gradual loss of excitement that accompanies the institutional loss of collective memory about why the change took place. I am reminded of comparisons of attitudes about the United States between newly naturalized citizens and those who were born here. It is striking to note how easily we adjust to the present modes, ignorant of or apathetic about the conditions that made the present both necessary and possible. Consider the rejuvenation of enthusiasm for the project. You must be mindful of the need to "pass the torch" to new keepers of the flame. Without intergenerational attention, the changes will pass from favor and be lost. In some cases, that may be proper. However, if you believe that your change is still important, you must take steps to ensure its longevity.

Gentle Pressure. If the change is important to you and the institution, make sure it manifests itself in everything you do. In all your memorandums, speeches, and meetings, keep a constant, gentle flow of information and pressure in favor of the new change. I recall a sailor telling me that the most gentle breeze can move the biggest ship if sustained long enough.

The Individual and Change

Personal Growth and Change. Individuals must change to grow. This is as true in a psychological as in a physical sense. However, change is always upsetting, and people therefore resist it. My parents often said, "I'm too set in my ways to change." Change causes conflict in the individual. On the one hand, each of us is excited by the prospects of certain changes (amusement park for children, a new car or boat for adults) and fears other kinds of change (a new school for children, a new job or community for adults). The change that we call personal growth usually comes about only after events have pushed us off our psychological equilibrium. Growth may ensue when we recover our stable platform.

Coherence. The notions of Carl Rogers (1980) about individuals had a great impact on my own consulting. His research shows that people are always striving to bring their feelings and actions into harmony. He calls this *coherence.* In his person-centered therapy he tried to help the individual bring about a better balance, finding that, all too often, we submerge our feelings and do not let them inform our actions, thus making our actions inappropriate or at least unhelpful. When we introduce change, we destroy or damage the balance between thoughts and actions for many affected persons. Old defense mechanisms may be brought into play as a self-protective action, resulting in resistance to or sabotage of the change.

Given an opportunity, people will bring greater coherence to their lives. If we, as change agents, are aware of this normal desire, we can encourage those affected by the change to focus on elements that seem to reduce personal coherence for them. We can also help them work through the anxieties they feel about the change and reduce their negative feelings. As a result, their lives can be brought into better balance, thereby freeing energy for the tasks at hand. A person's sense of self-worth is directly proportional to his or her ability to function competently. Greater coherence means having a better sense of self.

Transactional Analysis. An important element in our striving for coherence is the internal battle that each of us wages to balance the messages that we learned in early childhood. The field of transactional analysis (Berne, 1964) describes these learned messages and how they influence and often interfere in our dealings with others. Berne speaks of the messages we develop during childhood as being of two types. First, there are the creative, happy messages, which he has termed the *child.* Next are the nay-saying messages, which carry fear and restraint and the threat of punishment. These are termed the *parent.* Later, the growing child works to balance these conflicting messages with her or his new experiences, and Berne calls this third stage the *adult.* The basic responses that we give to others in any transaction, says Berne, are the result of one or another of these three ego states' being triggered during the transaction. As a result, we may react to change in a way that appears irrational to others because we have tapped some negative messages from our childhood. Berne makes an analogy to having a library of prerecorded tapes. A transaction or event causes one of these tapes to be played, and we must listen to it. We are not being really rational at such times but are merely reacting to some early emotional message. As these intrapersonal messages affect our relations with others, as inevitably they must, according to Berne, then we have a complex set of variables to consider in pressing for change in others. It is easy to watch a committee work and to quickly assess the present ego state of each member as he or she participates. If we are aware of the types of messages, often defensive, that we and others project on new situations, we can gain the sensitivity and skills needed to minimize the negative impact of such interchanges.

Habits, Routines, and Technologies. Every individual is confronted, minute by minute, with a dazzling array of visual, tactile, and auditory stimuli. We each process an enormous amount of information as we cope with our environment. Through evolution, we have developed many attributes that allow us to function in a seemingly smooth fashion, embedded, as we are, in a jerky hodgepodge of events over which we have no control. One of our principal adaptations is the ability to ignore that which is stable and concentrate on that which is moving or changing. Our eye is able to catch the smallest flutter of a bird's wing against a backdrop of trees. We cannot control our environment, but we can learn to assign parts of it to an unchanging status, leaving us free to deal with those parts that keep shifting.

The development of habits and routines is an attempt to bring order to a portion of our world. We can teach ourselves to perform various functions without thinking about them. Weisbord (1978) calls these routines technologies and likens them to the routines that we must perfect to operate some complex machine. The technologies we develop are tested and modified until they perform for us in the most efficient manner we can imagine. We then use them to free our attention for other considerations. We even extend these technologies to larger realms, making up operating theories that may encompass broad areas of work or involvement. In other words, our technologies or habits become clustered into larger frameworks, which we may think of as general modes of action.

Weisbord (1978), speaking about our habits/routines/technologies, reminds us that our technologies are not really autonomous. They involve exchanges of information, materials, people, and power. They involve feedback relations and feedforward situations. Most technologies are multifunctional in that they get both individual and group work done. We need to recognize that change requires individuals to break existing habits/routines/technologies and that the relationships between individuals must change as a result.

Theories in Use and Espoused Theories. Argyris and Schön (1974), by careful observation, have determined the patterns of thinking and work used by many different persons. A curious finding cropped up in their work when they asked individuals to describe their patterns or ways of thinking about a specific topic. The descriptions did not fit the observations. This was so generally true that the researchers came to differentiate between what they called a person's espoused theories and her or his theories in use.

Not only do individuals not do as they tell you they do; they are also unaware that their deeds do not fit their words. In other words, the espoused theories are created and maintained even though they are at variance with the theories in use. There are rather far-reaching consequences of this notion. According to Argyris (1982), when people say that they did not mean to act as they did, it can be inferred that this is a correct statement with respect to the espoused theory. However, it is not true for the theory in use.

It is commonly agreed that at any time a person is doing the very best that he or she can. This is in agreement with Rogers's (1980) ideas of coherence. Even when a person's actions seem to be counterproductive, as judged by someone else, the person being observed is using the most effective means at her or his disposal to address the current situation. We simply do not perform in ways that we know to be ineffective.

In the academic world, we place a high premium on the written word and on professional integrity. Therefore, we have a strong set of norms that cause us to take at face value the ex cathedra pronouncements of the professoriate. If it is found that such pronouncements represent espoused theories that bear only a passing resemblance to the actual modes of operation (theories in use), we have a big problem. I recall an instance where a new self-instructional learning program was being implemented. The provost was very supportive. A natural extension of the program allowed prisoners in the county jail to earn college credits in situ. This, too, was supported by the provost. Later, some prisoners who had served their time wanted to come to the campus to continue their education. The provost became so concerned about "that type of student" that the jail program was dropped. His espoused theory conflicted with his theory in use, and the latter won the day. Argyris states unequivocally that such is the case in virtually all organizational situations.

Many years after receiving my doctorate in biology, I appeared with an artist on a panel discussing the creative act in art and science. To the dismay of some, I took the position that the creative act was the same. I had come to realize that I did not approach science in the dispassionate manner discussed in textbooks, and neither did my research colleagues. We all espoused those ideas, but our theories in use were quite different. We were very emotional in defense of our ideas. We began new experiments based on intuition and feeling. We used our authority to control the opinions of "lesser lights." In short, we practiced not what we preached.

Argyris (1982) goes on to say that our theories in use are general designs that can be used to execute action in a given situation. They are like master programs, are not situation specific, and appear to have been learned early in life through socialization.

Striving for Consistency. Argyris concludes that people are fundamentally rational. To be rational means "(1) to intend to bring about certain consequences, (2) to have an explicit or tacit design or theory about how to accomplish one's intentions, (3) to act intentionally consistent with the design, (4) to feel a sense of success or failure, depending on whether one's intentions were achieved, and (5) to correct mismatches so that designs lead to a match between intention and outcome" (1982, p. 95). This is true of the theories in use. It certainly may not be true of the espoused theories. If we wish to know the theory in use, Argyris says, we must observe it.

We see a tie between Rogers's ideas of coherence and Argyris's notions of rational behavior. We need to remember that the individual is always striving, in his or her own way, for consistency of action and harmony with the immediate world. The fact that each individual has a different vision of what that harmony looks like means that our task as change agents is more difficult. What we have going for us is the notion that each player is really trying to bring order to her or his personal world of chaos. We can build on that sincere effort once we understand it.

The Group and Change

A committee or task force is a temporary, part-time collection of individuals. Each member brings all his or her assets and liabilities to the group. Given a group charge, each person will interpret that charge according to her or his set of theories in use but will discuss the charge in terms of her or his espoused theories. Thus, from the outset, the group is beset with mixed feelings and messages.

Given enough interaction time, group members begin to discover their colleagues' theories in use, even though these are not talked about openly. As the participants continue to work, the group begins to take on a life of its own—a metastructure. It will develop and use its own espoused theories and theories in use. One could develop a scale of attributes for a group that has been together for some time. There would be group norms about attendance, modes of presentation, deference to certain members, avoidance of certain topics, and even accepted level of levity. The group members bring their individual habits, which are tested in the group. The group develops a set of behaviors that are the resultant of all the individual behaviors.

If the group members possess approximately the same high degree of task orientation, they are less likely to be aware of each other's theories in use. When the charge to the group is to deal with a highly visible policy matter, individual members are likely to fall back on espoused theories to protect themselves, thus reducing the possibility for learning as a group.

Thus, both high task orientation and politically charged agendas will mean that the group is less likely to become a creative unit capable of producing novel and useful outcomes. For example, when a rural college was planning an urban campus in newly renovated space, a committee was chosen to deal with logistics. Members of the committee included the various academic division heads, the dean of continuing education, and persons from the plant department, budget office, and computer center. This highly motivated work group came up with recommendations that created a firestorm among the faculty. Infighting among departments over room assignments, numbers of assigned classrooms, and even parking spaces created chaos. Finally, a totally new set of committees was appointed, and much of the completed planning was scrapped.

Models for Change

The remainder of this chapter deals with two models for institutional problem solving. The first model is used by 95 percent of all committees on all campuses. Although it has limited utility for solving major problems, it is guarded and preserved because it grows out of our early conditioning as individuals. This model represents the distillation of the societal pressures of school, church, neighborhood, and job. It codifies the status quo and is highly resistant to change. The second model is not common but has great potential for improvement of institutional functioning. It requires a reorientation in the thinking patterns of its practitioners and runs counter to existing orthodoxy. Both models have been described in detail by Argyris (1982).

Argyris calls the first model *single-loop learning*, but I prefer the term *nonadaptive problem solving*. The essence of this model is that problems are addressed solely on the basis of currently accepted norms, attitudes, and beliefs. The result is that solutions that do not impact those individual, group, or institutional norms are proposed and implemented. The solutions may be useful or dysfunctional.

The second model, which Argyris terms *double-loop learning* (and which I call *adaptive problem solving*), also deals with problems but has as a stated group value the possibility for reexamination of norms, attitudes, and beliefs when the proposed solutions seem inappropriate or unworkable. According to Argyris, this second model is rarely used. However, it does have the benefit of giving significant information back to the organization. Therefore, its wider application would be beneficial.

Although Argyris's work is complex, there are a handful of key elements that are useful in comparing the two models and in relating them to our own body of experience. I will first present the basic features of the nonadaptive problem-solving mode and relate them to our "business as usual" way of group problem solving. I will then contrast the basic elements with the adaptive problem-solving overlay. It is my hope that you will be sufficiently intrigued by the adaptive problem-solving model to follow up with more study of Argyris's work.

Nonadaptive Problem Solving. Argyris (1982) says that people are predisposed to enact a world that values unilateral control, winning, suppression of negative feelings, and focus on rational behavior. First, he says, we use insufficient data collection. Second, we impose cultural biases on the data we have in hand, leading to the formulation of inferences that are flawed because they are based on bad data. Argyris believes we make untested inferences to cope with the complexity of our world. By making a model of a situation, we reduce the amount of specific information we must store and process. We may propose solutions based on our inferences, but they will be flawed for the same reasons.

Aside from these procedural flaws, we have been taught and conditioned to avoid confrontation. This avoidance is such a strong social rule, instilled from early childhood, that we are unable to overcome it except with vigorous attention. The socialization that limits our aggression is counterproductive to group change because we extrapolate nonaggression to mean "no hurt feelings," resulting in a limitation of the expression of feelings. We use "rational" behavior as the artificial substitute for "emotional" behavior and therefore fail to address issues of substance related to change because such issues would cause conflict among the participants. Finally, we are also taught that we must win. Our basic strategy for life is a win-lose proposition. Our own sense of security and self-esteem depends on reducing our vulnerability through control and winning.

Caught in situations where we must face value issues that challenge group norms, we react by distancing ourselves from the problem, deflecting the problem to others, and asserting that the conditions responsible for the problem are beyond our control. Borrowing from the individual theories in action of its members, the response of a group to vulnerability is self-protection, says Argyris (1982). As a result, our problem solutions become nonsolutions because they fail to address the fundamental issues. We create solutions that are dysfunctional and in the long run exacerbate the problems. This leads to recycling the major issues, with a resulting loss of momentum, energy, and desire for a solution. Frustrations grow as we fail to engage the primary issues.

The final result of this process is that we basically deny that the original problem really exists. We paper over the problem with sidestepping schemes. Argyris uses the term *camouflage* to describe these attempts to hide, disguise, or deny such problems. He maintains that the use of camouflage is the rule rather than the exception in any group.

The use of camouflage draws off energy that might otherwise be used to correct problems. Argyris goes on, "Moreover, when camouflage and protection are broadly practiced, they set the conditions for a second layer of camouflage. The hiding, denial, or disguising of uncorrectable error cannot come to light without actualizing this double layer of vulnerability. Hence, these procedures must be hidden, denied, or disguised" (1982, p. 93). He gives an example of a faculty committee charged with developing a set of recommendations for the president. The committee could not deal with the broad institutional issues in any concrete way without confronting the president's policies, so it presented a set of vague recommendations as its report. The president was unhappy with the recommendations but did not want to have a confrontation with the faculty, so he accepted the report and thanked the committee for its hard work.

The committee, because of its reluctance to face unpleasantness, was unable to deal with the critical issues in a constructive way, even though individual members might have had excellent ideas about how to truly bring about improvement. Rather than admit this inability, the group denied its problem and in so doing precluded the possibility of bringing about any true reforms. It then couched the report in language that made its vagueness appear to be a virtue, thereby adding the second layer of camouflage. Finally, as Argyris explains, the group denied that the process of covering up ever took place, thus sealing the process from any further investigation. This triple-layered system of denial operates in the vast majority of group undertakings, not only in higher education but also in all ventures.

According to Argyris (1982), we are conditioned to make such distancing moves beginning early in our lives. Our society is structured in a way that such distancing is reinforced, whereas openness (which sometimes includes negative feelings) is made suspect. As a consequence, we are left with a set of tools inappropriate for dealing with the tasks that our general organizational structures require.

A Personal Example. We defend our distancing by instituting punishments and penalties for probing that denial. I once felt the combined weight of disapproval from a group of highly respected educators. A number of years ago I was asked to work with a group of experienced college administrators in outlining a set of operating rules to be used by consultants new to the business. At my initial presentation to the group, I said that it was important, in addition to presenting the obvious practices that should be observed, to sensitize the new consultants to a range of problems they would face. My list of problems encompassed many of the concerns raised in this chapter. They dealt with the hidden agendas, the individual rivalries, the political power plays, and the expressions of vulnerability and unilateral control. I pointed out that new consultants, if aware of these problems, would be more helpful in getting the institution beyond such roadblocks and in facilitating forward movement.

All the members of the group attacked me and my ideas. They not only exhibited the denial Argyris talks about but also actively wanted to suppress my thinking on the matter. I remember statements such as "I would be embarrassed to bring up such matters." You can imagine the conclusion of that encounter. I wrote my report and turned it in. It was promptly rewritten in acceptable language and form by someone else, and the project proceeded. Denial was complete. The undiscussible was never discussed.

Since that encounter, my experience has shown me ever more strongly that Argyris is correct. It is disconcerting to think that much of the work we do goes unused because of distancing. There are some situations, however, in which the participants are truly interested in coming to grips with the problems facing them, even considering that institutional norms may have to change as a result and there are individuals who yearn for a more positive approach. You, as a change agent, can become skillful in assisting others in reducing denial and in promoting an adaptive group problem-solving effort.

In summary, then, the use of nonadaptive problem solving leads us to achieve our perceived purposes, maximize winning or minimize losing, avoid eliciting negative feelings, and be rational (minimize emotionality). Among the strategies used are unilateral control, protection of one's self, and unilateral protection of others. The consequences of this behavior are defensive interpersonal and group behavior, defensive norms, low freedom of choice/commitment/risk taking, little public testing of theories, and decreased effectiveness.

Adaptive Problem Solving. In sharp contrast to the foregoing, the basic principles of adaptive problem solving are advocacy, inquiry, surfacing of threatening issues, creation of disconfirmable statements, and public testing of inferences. A group practicing adaptive problem solving will be seeking to put effective functioning of the institution ahead of individual gains. Group members will understand that when issues of policy are involved, there may be a need to examine the basis on which the policy was formulated, collect data to test the efficacy of that policy, and potentially change the policy. There is a group norm allowing expressions of emotion. There is a recognition that rational thinking need not exclude emotional input. The group members will not feel threatened by emotional statements. Finally, the group can create statements of condition *that can be tested* and confirmed or disconfirmed—thus making the process truly cybernetic and self-correcting.

In applying these principles to a group process, we would start with a problem or charge to the group. Then the group would gather data, both statistical and anecdotal. After discussion, a range of possible solutions would be proposed. The probable impact of each solution within the group and without would be discussed.

Let us consider that the chosen solution would be in conflict with institutional espoused theory. For example, a college has an announced policy of increasing the diversity of its student body. This is understood to mean the admission of more minority students, persons from disadvantaged backgrounds, older students, and so on. At the same time the president feels that the institution should be raising its academic standards. A task force is formed to make recommendations for raising those standards. The committee studies the problem and determines that simply increasing the cutoff scores for incoming freshmen would raise the academic standards.

This creates a conflict with the policy of diversity because many of the "diverse" students have lower achievement scores on entering the school. Using adaptive problem-solving methods, the committee would open a discussion of the issues surrounding both the desire for greater diversity and that for improved academic standards. Both of these issues are invested with layers of self-interest, posturing, prestige issues, and financial considerations.

The committee, acting in this new mode, would probably ask that its charge be broadened so that it could deal with the range of relevant issues. It would institute campuswide inquiries about the rationale for each issue. It would probably spin off subgroups to deal with data collection. All these measures would bring to the surface the underlying issues with which so many fear to deal.

Solutions would be proposed which deal with both issues and might mean some changes in the stated goals of the institution. The proposed solutions would be put to the campus for discussion. Only after a thorough ventilation of feelings had taken place would any closure be sought.

Each of you can think of similar examples with which your institution deals every year. While the shift to adaptive problem solving will initially bring about turmoil, it can have very beneficial results for both the institution and the individuals involved. For the institution, there will be a decrease in dysfunctional group dynamics, a reduction in unrealistic organizational norms and activities, and an increase in changeability of systems. For the individual participants, there will be a decrease in double binds and an increase in true participation in policy making and congruence.

Argyris (1982) emphasizes that people in both models can be very articulate about their purposes and goals. However, the two models part company over the issue of control. Actors in nonadaptive problem-solving situations want to control others and the environment to ensure that they win. Adaptive problem solvers reject the idea of unilateral control and invite others to confront their views to bring about an action based on the most complete information possible. Argyris says, "Individuals [using adaptive problem solving] seek to build viable decision-making networks in which the major function of the group is to maximize the contributions of each member; when a synthesis is developed, the widest possible exploration of views has occurred" (1982, p. 103).

One of the most difficult aspects of adaptive problem solving is giving up our well-used strategies and learning a new set that will facilitate the new approach. Because change of the type we are hoping for means going against established cultural and social norms, we must deal with a process that ultimately will impact our everyday life as well.

To succeed with adaptive problem solving, we must go through periods when we have a sense of not being in control. However, Argyris says, "Being able to reflect on failure and lack of control is, paradoxically, the first step toward being in control" (1982, p. 455).

The way we begin to move toward adaptive problem solving is through a process that Argyris (1982) calls *unfreezing*. His reasoning goes like this: as a result of our unsuccessful actions and our unawareness, we feel decreasing self-confidence, an increasing sense of being out of control, and an increasing fear of not being in contact with reality, and therefore we feel vulnerable. If we deny our errors and believe that new actions are impractical, we will repeat the cycle over and over again.

If, in contrast, we inquire and confront others and reflect, experiment, and generate new models of theories in use, these will bring about new actions, new competence, just actions, and a growing sense of confidence, allowing us to continue the learning process.

A significant part of the vulnerability felt in this process has to do with the expression of feelings, with the realization that conflict with others will be highly probable. On the positive side, Argyris points out that "expressing feelings, however, uncovers more profound insights. People learn that along with feelings go reasoning processes that are rarely understood, partly because they are tacit and partly because they are smothered by the feelings" (1982, p. 170).

As experience is gained in adaptive problem-solving situations, the participants will realize that the distancing they traditionally use to make their immediate situations more tolerable actually leads to a "social pollution" that, according to Argyris, may make them feel like prisoners, leading an impossible life.

While it is probably not possible for any of us to rid ourselves of defensive behavior, we can strive to recognize such a posture and to quickly examine its roots. We can become skilled at rapidly analyzing our reasons for defensive behavior, often in time to take corrective action in the same conversation, thus reopening communication channels (Argyris, 1990). Argyris says, "As people become more skilled, they may actually take less time to act, because they can be clearer, more precise, and less cagey. Significantly less information is considered undiscussible, and fewer games are played to keep the undiscussible undiscussible. Organizations in which adaptive problem-solving occurs tend . . . to hold fewer or shorter meetings, because they can get to the difficult issues more quickly and because members do not need the meetings to keep one another appropriately informed (a euphemism for 'I'd like no surprises')" (1982, p. 180).

Adaptive Problem Solving and Liberal Learning. It has been suggested that the adaptive problem-solving model closely resembles the classical liberal arts model of education. The emphasis on the fearless pursuit of truth and beauty, the importance of inquiry and discourse, and the value placed on scholarship are all valuable to both liberal learning and adaptive problem solving. Let me voice a strong caveat, however. The classical liberal learning model is really an espoused theory. It has been handed down from generation to generation by faculty and students. As such, it is very easy to use the liberal learning model as an excuse for not applying the adaptive problem-solving model.

Remembering that it is our individual theories in use that must change in adaptive problem solving, we must question elements of the liberal learning model and subject them to the same scrutiny we do any other institutional policy. I do not think that adherence to the principles of liberal learning will help us achieve proficiency in adaptive problem solving. We must set aside the espoused theories, learn our new lessons, and only then seek application of the liberal learning principles.

Rogers, Berne, and Argyris. Let me end with a few statements that will tie together elements from the work of Rogers, Berne, and Argyris. Each author has a model to present. Each is concerned with human development. Each has worked to help individuals and groups use their potential for improving the human condition.

First, I see the group as an extension of the individual. Therefore, I believe that a group strives for coherence, just as does each participant. My experience in sensitivity training ("T" groups) has shown me that a collection of individuals, given time and a supportive atmosphere, can create a set of operating rules supportive of both group and individual needs. So Rogers and Argyris are talking the same language with respect to purposes. This striving for coherence is an overriding theme for all of us, and it is true regardless of the ego state (Berne's term) we are occupying at the moment. The child, parent, and adult ego states each attempts to bring coherence when it is in charge.

I believe that Argyris's ideas of espoused theories is congruent with Berne's parent ego state. The messages that we receive from parents (both biological and sociocultural) are largely framed in a cautionary context. There are more "don't's" than "do's." When we read any idealistic set of statements, whether religious, educational, or nationalistic, we can almost hear a voice saying, "Because if you don't . . ." Berne talks about both the disapproving parent and the petulant child as two conditions common in all of us. There is also the bargaining child who tries to placate the parent with promises of good works. I believe that many of our espoused theories represent this basic approach.

Adaptive problem solving calls forth both the child and the adult ego states. It is the child that is the creative part of us. Because this ego state is so fragile, it will not flourish except when given permission. Recall how brainstorming works. The leader tells the group that for a period of time (usually about five minutes) all suggestions will be considered. No judgments or negative comments are allowed. It is not a coincidence that such directions have to be stated. We have each spent a lifetime having our "child" trampled on by someone's "parent." The conditions that favor adaptive problem solving are the same ones used in any creative problem-solving process.

Finally, I believe that society strongly favors Berne's notions of child and parent. Because each person has parents, either real or surrogate, he or she has been the recipient of a barrage of restrictive messages. Our society is constructed to exercise control over the individual. All of our institutions, whether social, religious, or governmental, operate to extract a measure of control in return for whatever largess is provided. We are socialized to behave, conform, be team players, not be whistle-blowers, and so on. Society imposes strong sanctions on those who transgress its rules. It is little wonder that most groups distance themselves from unpopular situations; each member's "child" is retreating into the folds of the "parental" cloak.

Rogers, Berne, and Argyris have assembled an impressive body of knowledge about the human condition. The similarities of their findings gives credibility to the approaches that each uses to free us individually and enhance society through our collective action.

Your Next Step. As they say in sports, "The ball is in your court." If you wish to get your implementation job over as quickly as possible, continue to use the nonadaptive problem-solving approach and concentrate on the earlier parts of the chapter, which deal with the "what is." If, however, you are ready to for a new challenge, which might become a lifelong undertaking, pay more attention to the adaptive problem-solving ideas in the latter half of the chapter.

The consultants who have visited your campus have decided to grow beyond the confines of a single institution. They have worked to develop an expertise in dealing with people that matches their knowledge in a special discipline or area of management. The good consultant, like the good institutional manager, lives with her or his decisions for a long time. No advice is given lightly, and none should be so accepted.

The type of enlightened learning and group process that I support so strongly is not for everyone. You have to be the judge of its potential usefulness for you. Even if you wish to move in that direction, you may feel that your current situation prohibits such action. There is always tomorrow.

References

Argyris, C. *Reasoning, Learning, and Action: Individual and Organizational.* San Francisco: Jossey-Bass, 1982.

Argyris, C. *Overcoming Organizational Defenses: Facilitating Organizational Learning.* Needham Heights, Mass.: Allyn & Bacon, 1990.

Argyris, C., and Schön, D. A. *Theory in Practice: Increasing Professional Effectiveness.* San Francisco: Jossey-Bass, 1974.

Beckhard, R. *Organization Development: Strategies and Models.* Reading, Mass.: Addison-Wesley, 1969.

Berne, E. *Games People Play.* New York: Ballantine, 1964.

Birnbaum, R. *How Colleges Work: The Cybernetics of Academic Organization and Leadership.* San Francisco: Jossey-Bass, 1988.

Cleese, J., and Booth, C. *The Complete Fawlty Towers.* London, England: Methuen, 1988.

Rogers, C. *A Way of Being.* Boston: Houghton Mifflin, 1980.

Weisbord, M. R. *Organizational Diagnosis: A Workbook of Theory and Practice.* Reading, Mass.: Addison-Wesley, 1978.

Robert J. Toft is the publisher of a national newsletter, The Grant Advisor *(Linden, Virginia 22642). He has been a professor of biology at several colleges, a research physiologist at the Argonne National Laboratory, a program director at the National Science Foundation, and a consultant to a dozen colleges and universities, principally in the areas of alternative curriculum development and grantspersonship.*

Appendix: Suggested Readings

Holtz, H. *Choosing and Using a Consultant: A Manager's Guide to Consulting Services.* New York: Wiley, 1989.
While this book was written primarily for administrators in the business and government sectors, it contains useful insights for college administrators as well. Holtz covers such topics as problem identification, selection criteria, costs, and management issues.

Matthews, J. B. *The Effective Use of Management Consultants in Higher Education.* Boulder, Colo.: National Center for Higher Education Management Systems, 1983. (ED 246 825)
Matthews suggests guidelines for managing campus consultancies in four stages: exploring issues and problems, defining a working relationship, completing the work itself, and evaluating project effectiveness. Matthews's discussion of mutual roles and responsibilities is especially useful.

Pilon, D. H., and Bergquist, W. H. *Consultation in Higher Education: A Handbook for Practitioners and Clients.* Washington, D.C.: Council of Independent Colleges, 1979.
Probably the most comprehensive resource available on the topic, this book combines theory with practical, step-by-step advice, including sample forms and flowcharts.

Schein, E. H. *Process Consultation: Its Role in Organization Development.* Reading, Mass.: Addison-Wesley, 1969.
This short book has become a classic in organizational development. In it the author argues a convincing case for using consultants as process facilitators rather than as strictly content experts. The text contains many insights for using consultants effectively, most particularly problem definition.

Wergin, J. F. *Consulting in Higher Education: Principles for Institutions and Consultants.* Washington, D.C.: Association of American Colleges, 1989.
Findings of a comprehensive evaluation of consultation projects in twenty-six diverse institutions form the basis of these principles, presented as desiderata for good consulting practice, by both consultants and the colleges they serve.

INDEX

Nonadaptive problem solving, 86–89
North Central Association, 5, 11

Observation, by consultants, 68
One-page contracts, 45, 47, 49
Openness, and planned change, 71–72, 80
Organizational charts, 78
Outcomes assessment, 1
Outside opinion, value of, 16, 35
Ownership, and planned change, 71–72, 79

Parent ego state. See Ego states
Part-time consultants vs. full-time consultants, 9, 36
Passive-aggressive behavior, 80–81
Paton, S. M., 42, 53
Person-centered therapy, 82
Ph.D. degree-holders, glut of, 8
Physical plant maintenance, and consultants, 12
Pilon, D. H., 1, 2, 3–13, 15, 16, 20, 21, 31, 95
Planning, for action, 70–72
Political influences, at institutions, 77; consultants as, 16
Political model, 78
Presentations, of consultants, 39–40
Presidents: autocratic, 63–64; role of, in consultation management, 55–66
Preventing Students from Dropping Out, 8
Private colleges, small, 24–25
Private reports, of consultants, 61, 62
Problem definition, and consultants, 18–19, 32–33, 60–61
Process consultation, 18
Professional and Organizational Development Network (POD), 9
Program review, networks for, 28
Proposals: evaluating, 34; negotiating changes to, 42–43
Psychologists, as consultants, 6
Public reports, of consultants, 62
Purchase orders. See Retainers

Racial tension, and consultants, 12
References, of consultants, 38
Referrals, from Council of Independent Colleges, 27
Regional accrediting associations, 5
Rehnke, M. A., 1, 20, 23–29

Reports, by consultants, 45–49, 62–63, 68–69
Request for proposal (RFP), 33, 39, 41–42; writing of, 33–34
Retainers, firm, 49, 50–51
Retention, and consulting, 7–8
Revolving College Doors, 8
Rogers, C., 82, 84–85, 92–93, 94

Sanford, N., 67, 73
Schein, E. H., 15, 16, 18–19, 21, 95
Schön, D. A., 84, 94
Search consultants, 6
Seashore, C., 71
Section 89, of the Internal Revenue Code, 4, 11, 12
Sensitive investigations, by consultants, 17
Sexism, on campus, and consultants, 12
Shenson, H. L., 44, 53
Single-loop learning. See Nonadaptive problem solving
Small-group work, value of, 69. See also Groups, Task forces
State networks, 28. See also Networks
Stewardship, and change, 81
Strengthening Developing Institutions Program. See Title III
Success-after-graduation study, 68

Task forces: to effect change, 85–86; to select consultants, 33. See also Groups
Technical expertise, need for, 15–16, 23
Telephone-communications, and consultants, 12
Theories, in use vs. espoused, 84–85
Title III (Higher Education Act), 1, 7, 10, 25
Toft, R. J., 2, 21, 75–94
Townsend, R., 35, 40
Trade associations, for consultants, 31
Training, of personnel, by consultants, 8, 11
Transactional analysis, 82–83. See also Ego states
Trio Programs, 7

Unfreezing, 91
Up the Organization, 35
Ury, W., 42, 53

Verbal agreements, 45
Vitae, of consultants, 37

ORDERING INFORMATION

NEW DIRECTIONS FOR HIGHER EDUCATION is a series of paperback books that provides timely information and authoritative advice about major issues and administrative problems confronting every institution. Books in the series are published quarterly in Fall, Winter, Spring, and Summer and are available for purchase by subscription as well as by single copy.

SUBSCRIPTIONS for 1991 cost $45.00 for individuals (a savings of 20 percent over single-copy prices) and $60.00 for institutions, agencies, and libraries. Please do not send institutional checks for personal subscriptions. Standing orders are accepted.

SINGLE COPIES cost $13.95 when payment accompanies order. (California, New Jersey, New York, and Washington, D.C., residents please include appropriate sales tax.) Billed orders will be charged postage and handling.

DISCOUNTS FOR QUANTITY ORDERS are available. Please write to the address below for information.

ALL ORDERS must include either the name of an individual or an official purchase order number. Please submit your order as follows:
    Subscriptions: specify series and year subscription is to begin
    Single copies: include individual title code (such as HE1)

MAIL ALL ORDERS TO:
    Jossey-Bass Inc., Publishers
    350 Sansome Street
    San Francisco, California 94104

FOR SALES OUTSIDE OF THE UNITED STATES CONTACT:
    Maxwell Macmillan International Publishing Group
    866 Third Avenue
    New York, New York 10022